On the Vineyard

On the Vineyard

with photographs by Peter Simon

contributions by Evelyn Ames, Robert Brustein,
Nelson Bryant, Art Buchwald, Stanley Burnshaw,
Douglas Cabral, Peter Barry Chowka, Robert Crichton,
Stephen Davis, Nicholas Delbanco, Maitland Edey,
Ruth Gordon, Stan Hart, Henry Beetle Hough,
Garson Kanin, Maria Katzenbach, Daniel Lang,
Phyllis Méras, John B. Oakes, Vance Packard,
James Reston, Dionis Coffin Riggs, Wenonah V. Silva,
Anne W. Simon, Carly Simon, Red Smith,
Rose Styron, William Styron, John Updike,
Dorothy West and Marianne Wiggins

Anchor Books
Anchor Press/Doubleday, Garden City, New York, 1980

Peter Simon is a well-known free-lance photographer. Born in New York City in 1947, he grew up in the suburb of Riverdale and attended Riverdale Country School and the Fieldston School. While still in high school he worked as chief photographer for his local paper, the *Riverdale Press,* and published a camera magazine at his school. He received his formal photographic training while at Boston University, where he majored in photojournalism and graduated with a B.A. in 1970. He became photo editor of the *Cambridge Phoenix* in 1969, a position he held for a year before moving to a commune in Vermont. While there, he published his first book, *Moving On/Holding Still* (Grossman), in 1972. His second book, *Decent Exposures* (Wingbow Press), was published in 1974. He moved permanently to Martha's Vineyard in 1973, where he continues his free-lance work. A photobiography of his sister, *Carly Simon Complete* (Alfred A. Knopf), was released in 1975, and his most recent book, *Reggae Bloodlines* (Doubleday/Anchor), was published in 1977. His work has appeared in many other books and magazines, including *Life, Newsweek, Village Voice, Rolling Stone, New Times, High Times, New York Times Magazine, Atlantic Monthly, Popular Photography,* and *Crawdaddy.* Currently he is the photo editor of *New Age* and a staff photographer for the *Vineyard Gazette.* Peter has had many one-man shows, most notably at the Nikon House and Neikrug Gallery in New York, the Kiva Gallery in Boston, and the Field Gallery in West Tisbury.

Anchor Books Edition: 1980

We gratefully acknowledge permission to reprint:

"A Tree Grows in the Sand" by Nelson Bryant, *The New York Times,* 1973

"Private Beach: A Public Health Problem" by Art Buchwald, the Globe Library, 1978

"Procreations" by Stanley Burnshaw, reprinted by permission of the author and George Braziller, Inc., publishers of *In the Terrified Radiance,* 1972

"The Art of Loafing" by James Reston, the *Vineyard Gazette,* 1976

"A Mighty Angler Before the Lord" by Red Smith, *The New York Times,* 1977

"Lobsterville, Childhood, and Summer Days" by Dionis Coffin Riggs, the *Vineyard Gazette,* 1969

"Lambert's Cove" by Carly Simon, reprinted from a song called "Terra Nova" by Carly Simon and James Taylor. Used with permission from Carly Simon.

All photographs by Peter Simon except p. 81, p. 161, and the back cover by Ronni Susan Simon; p. 59 (top) and p. 167 by Alison Shaw; p. 123 by Richard Simon; and p. 79, courtesy of Connie Sandborn.

DEDICATION AND ACKNOWLEDGMENTS

On the Vineyard is a collaborative effort by many of us who live here. It is dedicated to the preservation of our land, sea, natural resources, and lifestyle. I wish to deeply thank all of the authors who were generous enough to contribute their work to this anthology. In addition, I'd like to give thanks and praise to various others who have also aided greatly in this project:

Ronni Susan Simon, my creative and supportive wife who has contributed three of her photographs to this effort. Ronni is also a key source of energy and inspiration for me.

Douglas Parker, who is responsible for the design of this book as well as three of my previous ones. He loves the Island so much, having been a constant year-round visitor for over a decade, that he recently bought a stately home and studio/gallery called *On the Vineyard* in Tisbury, near Tashmoo.

Stan Hart, author/bookstore owner, tennis champ, and wonderful person who helped me contact some of the authors included here, gave advice and consent throughout; and wrote some of the more humorous biographies.

Jon Nelson, owner of the other main bookstore on the Island who gave me invaluable ideas and guidance concerning format, reproduction, and marketing.

Douglas Cabral, former managing editor of the *Vineyard Gazette*, who helped enormously in editing the manuscripts, writing some of the short biographies after each piece, and who has been a pleasure to work with through all these years.

Angela Iadavaia-Cox, my editor at Doubleday. She has had to endure all of my idiosyncratic ways and bizarre demands, and even gave birth to a son during the production.

Connie Green, Angela's assistant who took over completely during Angela's maternal absences and skillfully handled many of the details that can be so problematic in book publishing.

Karen Mullarky, former picture editor at *Life, Rolling Stone,* and *Look.* Karen, who knows both my work and the Vineyard intimately, lent her expertise in both areas.

The ***Vineyard Gazette,*** our weekly small-townish newspaper that has the best newsprint reproduction I have ever dealt with. The ***Gazette*** has provided me with the inspiration and forum for producing these images, and has been a staple for most Islanders.

CONTENTS

1

THE LAST RESORT

by Peter Simon

7

PARACHUTE

by Maria Katzenbach

11

GOING BAREFOOT

by John Updike

21

THE GAY HEAD STORY

by Wenonah V. Silva

24

PRIVATE BEACH:
A PUBLIC-HEALTH PROBLEM

by Art Buchwald

27

IN PRAISE OF
VINEYARD HAVEN

by William Styron

29

CHAPPAQUIDDICK

by Vance Packard

32

THE VINEYARD'S
GRAPES OF WRATH

by John B. Oakes

35

A MIGHTY ANGLER
BEFORE THE LORD

by Red Smith

37

THE GOINGS-ON IN
MURIEL TOOMEY'S BACK LOT

by Robert Crichton

43

THE VINEYARD:
A MODERN LOVE AFFAIR

by Peter Barry Chowka

46

A TREE GROWS IN THE SAND

by Nelson Bryant

52

YOU CAN STILL CHOOSE
FOR THE VINEYARD

by Anne W. Simon

57

OFF-SEASON

by Douglas Cabral

65

UP-ISLAND JOURNAL

by Stephen Davis

79

THE LEGEND OF OAK BLUFFS

by Dorothy West

90
VINEYARD PASSAGE
by Robert Brustein

97
WHISKEY SOUR
by Daniel Lang

101
FOUR WILD TURKEYS
by Maitland Edey

105
WINTER SUITE
by Phyllis Méras

114
THANKSGIVING WALK
by Rose Styron

119
REPRISE
by Nicholas Delbanco

124
NOT FOR EVERYBODY,
THANK GOD!!
by Ruth Gordon

133
TO THE MEASURE OF MAN
by Garson Kanin

146
LOBSTERVILLE, CHILDHOOD,
AND SUMMER DAYS
by Dionis Coffin Riggs

144
PROCREATIONS
by Stanley Burnshaw

147
INTO THE FUTURE DARKLY
by Henry Beetle Hough

153
AND TO YOUR LEFT,
LADIES AND GENTLEMEN,
MY HOUSE!
by Marianne Wiggins

156
THE ART OF LOAFING
by James Reston

162
CIRCLES IN TIME
by Evelyn Ames

171
NO EXIT FROM EDEN
by Stan Hart

182
LAMBERT'S COVE
by Carly Simon

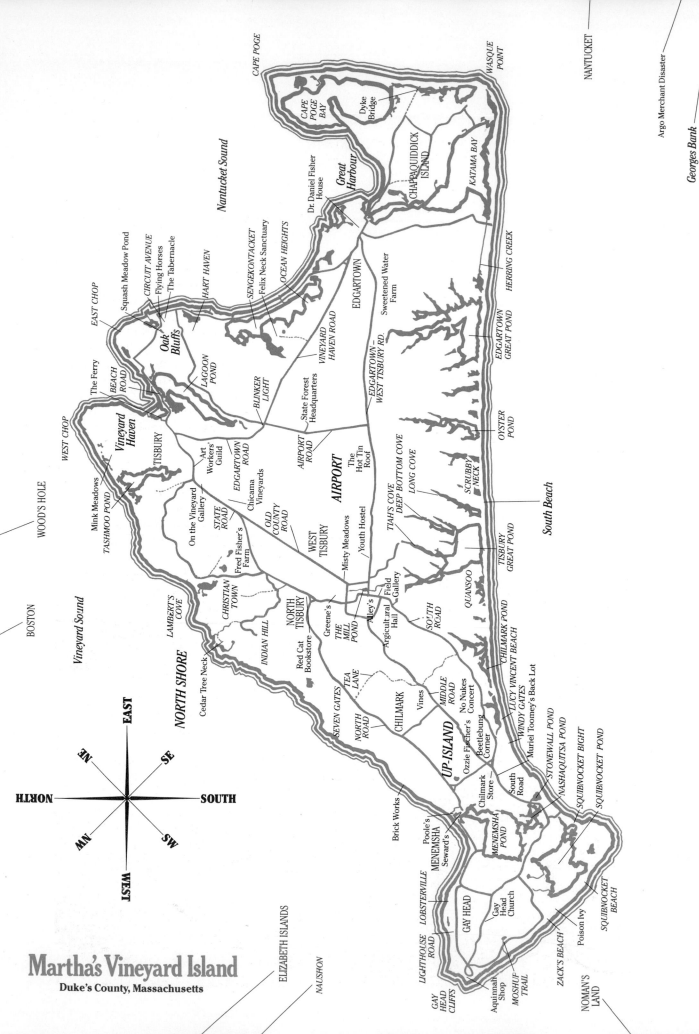

Martha's Vineyard Island

Duke's County, Massachusetts

THE LAST RESORT: AN INTRODUCTION

Peter Simon

So **many** of the people who live on the Vineyard or have visited even just once have a special feeling of love and connectedness for/to it. Despite all the problems that Vineyard life presents, we persist in returning here day after day, summer after summer, year after year. While living on the Vineyard as a mostly year-round resident for nearly ten years, I have been gradually photographing every element of the Island that presents itself to me; every vista, season, the many remarkable birds that choose to rest here, the gray shingled homes, the changing seascapes, the annual invasion of tourists and summer regalia, the cliché slices of Americana that float by my viewfinder; all the images so uniquely Vineyard. And even though the Island is only eighteen miles long and twelve miles wide — and although I have passed the same sights a million times — I've never tired of photographing it. I now have all these stored-up images I wish to share with those who feel the same sense of oneness with the Vineyard.

But my photographs depict only a certain vision of the Island — mostly an idealistic one. I have trouble pointing my lens toward the tackiness of Beach Road in Vineyard Haven, the condominiums of Katama, or the boring tour buses and mopeds that clog up the winding, narrow up-Island roads in the heat of summer. Nor do I tend to see images of Islanders in a freaky, Dianne Arbus-type perspective. I could take those kinds of images anywhere, and have. But, the idyllic country charm of the *Vineyard Gazette* has mellowed many of my biting, satiric inclinations of ages past. In addition, Martha's Vineyard presents such a wide spectrum of people, lifestyles, and various scenarios of one kind or other

Windy Gates seascape, autumnal sky

that it would be an impossible task to try to show it all, much less be witness to it. Thus the photographs in this book attempt to give an overall (and occasionally specific) picture of what life on the Vineyard is all about, without the burden of being totally comprehensive or needlessly jaded.

On the other hand, I wouldn't want this book to be merely pleasant propaganda for this endangered island, which already has enough media attention and tourist attraction. The book needed a good, hard-hitting text for a proper balance. But who should be the author? I realized that the Vineyard is blessed with so many gifted writers who take refuge here, that to narrow it down to one would be a

The Horsewoman

mistake. Through the years of living here, I have had the pleasant occasion of meeting a large number of Island authors. Some have become close friends, others warm acquaintances. Still others I never met, but knew of and respected from afar, or heard of through the grapevine. One by one I contacted them to survey their interest in a possible contribution to an anthology about our Island. To my great pleasure, almost everyone appeared quite enthused over the project, and agreed to the task. Because I felt that one third of the royalties of this book should go to a deserving Island charity, everyone agreed to write their essay without payment. That's true love! I asked each contributor to write a short, free-form essay on any subject, as long as it dealt with the Vineyard. I

suggested topics to a few writers who asked for guidance. And I chose a few others because they happened to be experts on certain aspects of Vineyard life. As word of this project got out, the list of authors started expanding, until finally I had to put the cap on it. It was a hard process of elimination. There are many Island authors not represented here, but we have tried to portray a fair sampling. Overall, after the pieces were in, I was impressed that a fairly random solicitation would result in such a well-rounded text, embracing a network of coverage and feelings.

Adapting my photographs to the treasury of words in hand became the next

Overlooking Seth's Pond

task. I reviewed literally hundreds of thousands of images from my negative file that I have captured through the years. All the memories came flashing back day after day: classic beach days, bizarre *Gazette* assignments, walking on sunsets, excursions to Chappaquiddick, the planting of the garden, my marriage to Ronni, a myriad of social gatherings, softball games, street fairs, the annual illumination night in Oak Bluffs, and various special Island occurrences such as the Chilmark picnic of July 4, '76, the No-Nukes Festival of early fall '78, the furiously cold and ice-clogged winter of '77, opening night at "The Hot Tin Roof," and the memorable day that a kilo of hashish washed up on the shores of Windy Gates, to

Menemsha sunset, looking toward the Elizabeth Islands

the astonishment of a handful of beneficiaries.

After all that printing and reminiscing, I wound up with a stack of prints two feet deep. The process of selection was overwhelming. A few became top priority simply because I considered them my best. Other images referred specifically to the text and were natural illustrations. Other shots were borderline cases that eventually were edited out. Some photographs I was particularly attached to for sentimental reasons were considered too banal or idiosyncratic by my wife and art director. And slowly, the final product began to emerge like a print in the developer.

The various contributing authors have said it all more gracefully than I ever could, but I will try anyway, in short. Aside from the many pleasures of living here, there are problems. The specter of overdevelopment is real — here, there, and everywhere. The fact that we live thirty-five miles from a nuclear reactor in Plymouth makes me feel quite vulnerable, more so than I am to natural disasters such as hurricanes (which I actually get excited about). The Navy uses a small island near us, "Noman's Land," for military bombing practice, which is quite jarring. Prices here for everything are high. We must pay for the "privilege" of being here. This is mostly due to the import situation, but also to an elitist, resort psychology. Elitism can run rampant, and many of us cause it. We live here and think we should keep it for ourselves exclusively — one of humanity's less evolved, self-protective instincts, yet a geographical reality. We have to rely on the capricious Steamship Authority for practically everything. And it's usually a struggle to get off and on; a rare pleasure when the day is sunny and calm with only a few passengers. Tick season is almost unbearable. Poison ivy is prevalent. The summers are too short and condensed. The rest of the year is full of holes. Cultural stimulation in winter is not really happening, except in one's own backyard. As a free-lance photographer, I have trouble making a career on the Island. All of my big-city colleagues get the juicy assignments, while I do local portraits, town meetings, or an occasional Vineyard happening that is big enough to make the newsweeklies. That's not quite enough to keep me afloat creatively or financially.

I could live here as many other "summer people" do, and might eventually as my city urges well up. Yet, so far, the unyielding sense of belonging and commitment I have to this place keeps me here most of the time. When I observe the conditions under which much of this world is forced to live, I chide myself for being spoiled enough to complain about the things I just mentioned.

I have traveled to exotic places, and have lived various different lifestyles in the past, but have never felt so at peace as I do as a Vineyarder. I feel as though I have escaped the craziness of the "real world," and am living out some sort of dreamy fantasy, where the elements I value most are all anchored firmly on this sea and soil. The Vineyard is the last resort for me, the only resort, at least for now.

It is the unique coming together of all the aspects of this island existence that allows us to cherish the land and way of life that the Vineyard still affords. Times are changing, but the Vineyard lags pleasantly behind. I dedicate this book to its preservation. *On the Vineyard* is an ode and a means to savor what we have mutually discovered.

Peter Simon   November, 1979

The famous pie-eating contest at the Chilmark Picnic, 1976

Morning comes to
the Mill Pond in West Tisbury.

A Gay Head perch for sunset

PARACHUTE
Maria Katzenbach

I am four. Five. Six. Counting. Learning smells and sights by name. Squibnocket: sand knobbly with rocks; where stars are tossed up from the ocean and are fish. Menemsha: a harbor; sounds like the kind of word a woman (opening her arms) says to a man. Pond is where I can swim without my father. Ocean is where I cannot swim without my father. Gay Head: earth celebrating itself; a festival at sunset; cliffs riotous in stripes every day, not just August. August: Ferris wheel, merry-go-round, horses, and chickens; August: too short. Poole's is a man with a profile unlike anyone else's. A pipe belongs to it. Poole's is a smell not found on humans or beasts. We get monsters called lobsters there. My mother dyes them red in steaming water on her birthday.

Flying Horses means that it is a rainy day. Vineyard Haven means we have arrived. Edgartown I feel I must tiptoe through (houses like just rinsed china). Oak Bluffs is doll houses overgrown.

There are words pointing to directions. West Tisbury is going south. South Beach is against the wind. Up-Island is *below* down-Island on the map. There is no north because north is snow and I believe that it never snows on Martha's Vineyard. Martha: a mermaid, a Viking princess, the first President's wife, the baby sitter my brother has his first crush on. The Vineyard has no vines. A harvest of beachplums and blueberries from an island. Island: land separated from land by ocean. A place that belongs only to itself.

Everett Poole

One morning one summer (the summer my brother tamed a baby hawk he called "Squawk") we awake and look outside to see what the weather will be. In the lone tree of the field that is the backyard, where sheep are nuzzling the grass, a parachute hangs. White, strings flying, it looks like the tree's sail half unfurled; like a cloud that wanted to hug something; like the sheet for the bed

"Flying Horses"— Oak Bluffs' pride and joy

of the tree. Wind catches up the silk and loops it around the largest branch of the tree. Then it subsides. It now looks like a curtain. The sheep (finally) notice it. They baa.

The parachute bellows back. The sheep baa at it as they run in the other direction. The parachute bellows again. It tangles and twists itself without any help from the wind, bellowing and snorting. It is an angry god declaring war in the field — against sheep, summer people, invaders. We are trespassers on sacred ground. The sky god has come down, disguised as a parachute.

The god shows his head through the curtain. A black-and-white marbled crown, two horns, peeks through and rolls his eye. Zeus. As a bull (of course). He bellows. He stomps his hoof. He shreds the parachute.

We nominate our hero. Adopting the god's method, he goes down on hands and knees and baas his way through the sheep. The bull shakes his head at the beast in khakis and plaid shirt. His horns shrouded, he awaits him. Then the strange baaing beast rises on two legs (the audacity of him, thinks the god) and comes near. The bull snorts. Then, docile toward his rescuer, he submits to the delicate removal of the parachute.

The bull (no longer god) flicks his tail and wanders back home (the neighboring farm). Our hero teases him with the parachute playing matador. Nothing persuades the bull to go near it.

The rest of the parachute remains on the tree, shredded by days and weather. We never come up with an explanation as to how it landed there in the first place.

It is summer again and I am eleven. (I say I am

*You don't need
a weathervane to know
which way the wind
blows.*

thirteen.) The first language of sight and smell wants to be formalized (made grown-up) on the page. I leave our house early one morning with an enormous straw bag. It is packed with three notebooks (I think a novel can be written in one morning), five pens, and two real books (one by Nicholas Delbanco). The day is overcast (too windy to be womby). I walk down the path to Baldwin's Beach. (The summer before, an infant was nursed there.) I expect the same waves (velvet clay) and sand (brushed fine) as the summer before. Standing at the top of the rickety stairs (high; the cliffs have not yet shed their first layer and dropped a sheath of history into the ocean), I look down. Rocks. There is no softness or luxury.

This is my first lesson in the art of writing.

I sit on a hard nest (my second lesson), my pages blank. I write nothing. I listen to the rhymes in the waves and the song the ocean is singing, trying to learn another language the Vineyard is offering me. It is called poetry and it dances.

Dancing. Four young women holding hands as they walk through the swampy path to Jungle Beach. The clouds breaststroke over the moon. Branches are breathing in the light. Each branch is the boa constrictor that has been let loose. (It is a rumor and we believe it.) We are singing hymns against the serpent. Branches coil; drop; writhe. The stench of mud gives way to the ocean's salt. The cliffs shield us from our own fear. All four women crowd on top of the large rock. We are Sirens singing Ulysses to us.

There are no more starfishes on Squibnocket. Traffic, taxis, bicycles, delays are Vineyard Haven when we arrive (at last). Near to where the sky god landed, jets land regularly. The jungle of Jungle Beach has been cleared out and the swamp has been filled in. Dancing is now performed for an audience and I have reviewed the dancers in the *Gazette.* It is the first time my prose has been in print. The topography of the Vineyard has been cut and edited and twisted around by Universal Studios.

The Vineyard organizes to secede.

It has already seceded. Language here is what you can touch. The waters sing to each muscle of your body and the dancers still transform the beach and the fields into a stage. Dancers climb to the moon, and the cliffs at Gay Head celebrate their own flesh every day at sunset.

And no one has explained the parachute.

The Vineyard has been the one constant place for Maria Katzenbach in a life spent moving around. Her first novel, The Grab *(1978), achieved great critical success, particularly in light of her age (twenty-four). Before that, she was a dance critic for the* Vineyard Gazette *(in 1974). She is now at work on a second novel, which is set on the Vineyard.*

The mainland takes over.

The Gay Head cliffs
at sunset.

Going barefoot

GOING BAREFOOT
John Updike

When I think of the Vineyard, my ankles feel good — bare, airy, lean. Full of bones. I go barefoot there in recollection, and the island as remembered becomes a medley of pedal sensations: the sandy rough planks of Dutchers Dock; the hot sidewalks of Oak Bluffs, followed by the wall-to-wall carpeting of the liquor store; the pokey feel of an accelerator on a naked sole; the hurtful little pebbles of Menemsha Beach and the also hurtful half-buried rocks of Squibnocket; the prickly weeds, virtual cacti, that grew in a certain lawn near Chilmark Pond; the soft path leading down from this lawn across giving, oozing boards to a bouncy little dock and rowboats that offered another yet friendly texture to the feet; the crystal bite of ocean water; the seethe and suck of a wave tumbling rocks across your toes in its surge back down the sand; sand, the clean wide private sand by Windy Gates and the print-pocked, overused public sand by the boat dock that one kicked around in while waiting for friends to be deferried; the cold steep clay of Gay Head and the flinty littered surface around those souvenir huts that continued to beguile the most jaded child; the

startling dew on the grass when one stepped outside with the first cup of coffee to gauge the day's weather; the warmth of the day still lingering in the dunes underfoot as one walked back, Indian-file, through the dark from a beach party and its diminishing bonfire. Going to the post office in bare feet had an infralegal, antitotalitarian, comical, gentle feel to it, in the days before the postal service moved to the other side of Beetlebung Corner and established itself in a lake of razor-sharp spalls. (When Bill Seward ran the postal annex in his store, it was one of the few spots in the United States that delivered mail on Sundays.) Shopping at Seward's, one would not so carefreely have shelled out "island prices" for such luxuries as macadamia nuts and candied snails had one been wearing shoes; their absence, like the cashless ease of a charge account, gave a pleasant illusion of unaccountability. A friend of mine, who took these photographs, used to play golf at Mink Meadows barefoot. My children and I set up a miniature golf course on a turnaround covered with crushed clam shells; after treading this surface for a while, it did not seem too great a transition, even for a middle-aged father of four, to climb a tree barefoot or go walking on a roof. The shingles possessed a pleasantly peppery, sunbaked sting.

These are summer memories, mostly August memories; for that's the kind of resident I was. Now it has been some summers since I was even that,

An extraordinary achievement

Jungle Beach

and a danger exists of confusing the Vineyard with my children's childhood, which time has swallowed, or with Paradise, from which we have been debarred by angels. Let's not forget the rainy days, the dull days, the cranky-making crowding, and the moldy smell summer furniture gives off when breezes don't blow through the screen door one keeps meaning to fix. Beach pebbles notoriously dry to a disappointing gray on the mantel. The cozy roads and repeated recreations can begin to wear a rut. One wet summer we all, kids and cousins and friends of cousins, kept walking down through poison ivy, *not* barefoot, to look at a heap of large stones that was either a ninth-century Viking cromlech or a nineteenth-century doghouse, nobody was certain which. Still, there was under everything, fair days and foul, a kicky whiff of freedom, a hint, whispered from the phalanges to the metatarsals, from the calcaneus to the astragalus, that one was free from the mainland's paved oppressions.

Going barefoot is increasingly illegal, and does have its dangers. One house we rented overlooked Menemsha Bight from a long porch whose spaced boards had the aligned nicety of harp strings or the lines of type in a book. One of

my boys, performing some stunt on these boards, rammed splinters into the soles of his feet so deeply a doctor across the island had to cut them out with a surgeon's knife. I wonder if even the most hardened hippies still pad along the tarry streets of Oak Bluffs barefoot as they used to. At Jungle Beach, I remember, nudity spread upward to the top of the head and became doctrinaire. But then nudism, interwoven with socialism in the island's history, has always had a doctrinaire side. Being naked approaches being revolutionary; going barefoot is mere populism. "Barefoot boy with cheek of tan" was a rote phrase of my own childhood, quaint even then. But that boy existed and can be seen, not only in illustrations of Mark Twain but also in Winslow Homer's level-eyed etchings and oils of his contemporary America, a place of sandy lanes and soft meadows. There are few places left, even summer places, where one can go barefoot. Too many laws, too much broken glass. On Long Island, the cuffs of one's leisure suit will drag on the ground, and on the Cape, pine needles stick to the feet. Even on Nantucket, those cobblestones are not inviting. But the presiding spirits of Martha's Vineyard, willfully and not without considerable overhead, do preserve this lowly element of our Edenic heritage: treading the earth.

Uphill footprints

John Updike is one of America's foremost writers. Born in 1932 in Shillingham, Pennsylvania, he graduated from Harvard as a member of the famous class of '54. He worked for two years for The New Yorker, *where many of his shorter pieces appear regularly. Since 1957 he has been a free-lance writer and novelist living on the North Shore of Massachusetts. His Vineyard life is mostly confined to occasional summer rentals in Chilmark, where he and his family vacation. His long list of acclaimed novels includes* Rabbit Run, Couples, Rabbit Redux, The Centaur, *and most recently,* The Coup.

John Updike, up on the roof

Taking a stand

*Mid-afternoon
space-out at
Menemsha*

A Sunday at Seward's

A warm summer rain enhances this view of Stonewall Pond.

Menemsha panorama as seen from West Basin

Jungle Beach vision

Cliffs made of clay

The Gay Head Cliffs suffer from the pounding surf of a summer gale.

A hidden pasture

THE GAY HEAD STORY
Wenonah V. Silva

Gay Head is the westernmost town on Martha's Vineyard. Called "Aquinnah" by the natives of Noepe (the Indian name for Martha's Vineyard), it is one of two Indian communities in the state of Massachusetts. It was incorporated as a town in 1870, ostensibly to improve the lot of the native Americans.

Prior to this time, these people owned all of the land communally, enjoying a culture distinct from that of their neighbors, sharing the land and its products as had their forefathers for hundreds of years.

When the "advantage" of becoming a township was discussed, the Indians circulated a petition, requesting that they remain as they were, lest they lose their identity. Twenty-five persons does not seem a significant number, it may well have represented all of the people of the day who could read or write. Formal education was, after all, not a prerequisite for their survival.

When the town was incorporated, the land was divided among people living in the former Indian district, according to the state census of 1870. A few non-Indian people were given property, purportedly in settlement of a debt or for such services as surveying, an irony since they were, after all, unwilling partners in the luckless fate that befell them.

For the most part, the natives were self-sufficient. They utilized the natural products of the land, the wild growth of fern and flora, fish and game, cultivating crops, keeping modest herds of livestock or chickens, and exchanging these things for that which they could not produce themselves. Living was relatively simple for these resourceful, artistic, and inventive people. They were in great demand on seagoing vessels because of their knowledge of the water and weather, and resisted all efforts to change their way of life, regarding outsiders with suspicion. Also, they were insulated until a short time ago by geographical location, and by a network of ponds that provided a natural boundary between the towns of Gay Head and Chilmark. The Indians have continued their way of life in varying degree up to the present day.

There have been, however, outside forces challenging their heritage. Acceptance of religious influence and Christianity helped erode language and lifestyles common to the Indians. For example, while the Wampanoags language was spoken by the elders of the Gay Head community at the turn of the century, after a generation of contact with the dominant culture and influence of well-intentioned Church members, the language was eradicated except for isolated words and phrases.

Traditions have been lost too, such as one peculiar to the Gay Head Wampanoags, the celebration of "Cranberry Day." It was said to have been observed on the second Thursday of October, and was the first day of the cranberry harvest. Although in the past the native people have never been bound to the calendar, but rather have observed signs of weather and season, still no one now living remembers it ever having been observed on any other day.

All of the native people gathered on the cranberry bog, arriving by oxcart to pick the crop of wild cranberries. They shared a lunch of fried chicken and other home-cooked delicacies, usually topping off the meal with squash pie. In the days long past, they built bonfires and sang and danced into the night.

Indian crafts attract visitor's attention.

In 1972, led by a member of one of the foremost families in the Indian community, the Wampanoag Tribal Council sued the town of Gay Head for the return of their common lands. The common lands comprised about 230 acres of coastal property; the cranberry bogs, Herring Creek, and the face of the Gay Head cliffs. Surviving the first skirmish in an inevitably long court battle in federal court, the Tribal Council, representing the native American people, and the Gay Head Taxpayers' Association, representing the non-Indian taxpayers in town, stiffened for a lengthy court fight. Some townfolk, however, concerned with the detrimental effects of lengthy court sessions, and the economic devastation it would have on the town, sought to have the differences resolved in mediation.

The greatest problem that existed throughout the talks was the difference in the concept of land ownership between the native Americans and the whites. Long years of learning the traditions of their people will not be changed overnight. But surely after 300 years of living peaceably with non-Indians, a settlement that is acceptable to both sides must be worked out.

Whether viewed at the height of the summer season, or in the dead of winter, Gay Head has a unique and undeniable beauty. Increasing numbers of people have come to Martha's Vineyard to "see the sights." Not the least among these are the famed Gay Head cliffs, magnificent beyond description. Treks began in the nineteenth century, when tourists were induced to take a vessel to the North Shore, landing at Gay Head, where natives with teams of oxen took them along winding roads to the top of the cliffs. Here the tourists could view the cliffs in all their splendor. Here they rose in rugged ribbons of red, white, gray, yellow, and black clay 150 feet above the sea. Later in this century, they would be declared a national landmark.

Erosion has always been a problem with the cliffs area. Long periods of rain, natural springs of the purest water located in the cliffs area, the action of freezing and thawing during the winter months, and their location on the northwestern tip of the Island, where wind, weather, and tidal action combined to contribute to the problem, have done their utmost to diminish their size. Even the U. S. Corps of Engineers could offer no real solution to the problem. But in spite of the cliffs' diminishing size and color, more tourists than ever journey to Martha's Vineyard to see the cliffs.

The Wampanoags' legendary chieftain, Moshup, and his wife, Olesquant, are said to frequent the area. On foggy days, 'tis said, you can see him smoking his pee-auddleedee (pipe) among the dunes on the South Shore. And, if you listen as the night gathers, you can hear Olesquant sing a lullaby

*Napolean Madison,
chief medicine man.*

Thelma Weissberg, Gay Head's most outspoken advocate of the Wampanoag land claim suit, was greeted one morning by this spectacle in her mailbox. Indicative of the tension which occasionally exists in Gay Head, it is thought that the deerhead was a symbolic protest against her militant attitude, which has stalled a more moderate settlement.

One of Gay Head's oldest homes

to her children.

My father was Chief Medicine Man Napolean Madison (Squsin Wasquat: Red Hickory), and my mother was Nannetta C. W. Vanderhoop Madison, whose grandmother bore the Indian family name that I carry. My mother named me Wenonah, which means first-born daughter; Occoch, our family name; Madison, my maiden name; Vandal and Silva, names that I took in two marriages. My pride in my family history and heritage was taught by my mother, a teacher in her lifetime, who was concerned with the erosion of our Indian culture.

And as our search for "roots" becomes more popular, so does this pride increase among all our people.

Wenonah V. Silva, a soft-spoken, reflective woman, is a Wampanoag Indian who lives in Gay Head. She is a former president of the Indian Tribal Council, and a teacher, lecturer, and historian. She has written for the Vineyard Gazette *and for national publications edited for teachers. Indian arts and crafts are her preoccupations.*

PRIVATE BEACH:
A PUBLIC-HEALTH PROBLEM
Art Buchwald

My good friend Professor Heinrich Applebaum has just done a sociological study on how private beaches affect the average American's vacation. He did it under a grant from the "Life Is Unfair Foundation."

Applebaum's study came to some startling conclusions.

"You would think," he told me, "that people who own their own beaches would be twice as happy as those who don't."

"That certainly figures," I said.

"Well, it's not true. My interviews indicate that those who have no rights to a private beach are three and a half times happier than those who do."

I was certainly surprised.

He said, "It appears that those who don't own beach-front property believe the ocean is public and they have the right to use any beach they want to, even if it's marked "Private." In fact, they prefer to use a private beach more than they do a public beach because not only are private beaches nicer but also it drives the owners up the wall."

"I should think so. A person with a private beach has paid through the nose for it and he doesn't want just anybody using it. There are still such things as property rights in this country."

"Public bathers don't believe this," Applebaum

Beachgoers wishing to occupy the once-public Zack's Cliffs area are now confronted with this eyesore.

The beaches belong to the people?

said. "They feel that a beach is a beach is a beach, and if they can get away with using a private beach rather than a public one, their day is made. This is particularly true of nude bathers, who will walk miles across dunes, sand, and rocks to camp on a piece of property that is off-limits to them."

"That's terrible."

"It's worse than that. I discovered in my studies that as the summer goes by the owners of private beaches start suffering severe mental problems, including depression, paranoia, and hysteria. Very few of them can cope with strangers using their beaches. At the end of the summer they are psychological wrecks."

"How so?" I asked.

"Well, they get up in the morning, and the first thing they do is go down to their beach to see if anyone is on it. The thing about private beaches is people use them not only for sunbathing in the daytime, but also at night for other things. If they find their beach has been used at night, it drives the owners crazy. 'Get off my beach!' they scream at the people wrapped in their blankets.

"Then the beachowners go back to their houses to have breakfast. After breakfast they go back to the beach to see who is on it. If no one has arrived yet, they go into town to buy the papers and shop

A scene at one of the Vineyard's few public beaches

for groceries. But they are very ill at ease because all the time they're away they keep wondering if anyone is on their sand.

"When they return from town, they immediately go back to the beach to check it out. They sit on a sand dune waiting for the invaders. Some people send their children down to stand guard, and at the first sign of an unauthorized bather the children sound the alarm and everyone goes down to the beach to drive the trespassers off. If the sunbathers refuse to move, they have to go back to the house to call the police. This can kill two or three hours."

"It doesn't sound like much fun for the beachowners," I said.

"It isn't. They can't accept lunch dates or go fishing or sailing because they believe as soon as they go someone will walk on their property."

"A person could develop a complex after a while."

"Most of them do," Applebaum said. "They have nightmares, hallucinations, and crying jags. They start talking to themselves. And in some cases they even plot murder. If these people don't get treatment, they can become a danger to society."

"Then on the basis of your study you're recommending that people who own waterfront property seek psychiatric help as soon as the summer is over."

"It's essential," Applebaum said. "A person who owns a private beach at a summer resort is a walking time bomb that could go off at any moment."

Fortunately for Art, his land stops short of Vineyard Haven Harbor.

Art Buchwald summers in Vineyard Haven. The nationally syndicated humorist takes time from his tennis game occasionally to outrage Islanders with suggestions that a bridge ought to be built from the Island to the mainland, or a subway, better yet. Or he turns his bizarre sense of fun on Chilmark cannibalism. Once he suggested that everybody vacation on Nantucket instead.

Main Street, Vineyard Haven — only a bit tacky

*Getting through the ferry confusion in
Vineyard Haven.*

IN PRAISE OF VINEYARD HAVEN

William Styron

Once at a summer cocktail party in Menemsha I was asked by a lady: "Where on the island do you live?"

"In Vineyard Haven," I replied.

She suddenly gave me a look that made me feel as if I harbored a communicable disease. "My God," she said, "I didn't think anyone *lived* there."

Well, people do live there, and the moment of the year that I look forward to with unsurpassed anticipation is when I roll the car off the ferry, negotiate the fuss and confusion of the dock area, wheel my way past the homely façade of the A & P, twist around down Main Street with its (let's face it) unprepossessing ranks of mercantile emporia, and drive northward to the beloved house on the water. On an island celebrated for its scenic glories, Vineyard Haven will never win a contest for beauty or charm; perhaps that's partly why I love it. The ugly duckling gains its place in one's heart by way of an appeal that is not immediately demonstrable. The business district is a little tacky, but why should it be otherwise? It is neither more nor less

inspiring than other similar enclaves all across the land. People often think they yearn for quaintness, for stylishness, for architectural harmony; none of these would be appropriate to Vineyard Haven, which thrives on a kind of forthright frowsiness. A few years ago an overly eager land developer — now mercifully departed from the island — was heard proclaiming his desire to transform downtown Vineyard Haven into a "historical" site, similar to the metamorphosis effected by Mr. Beinecke on Nantucket. It is good that this plan came to naught. How silly and dishonest Cronig's and Leslie's drugstore would look wearing the fake trappings of Colonial Williamsburg.

As for residential handsomeness, the good town of Tisbury cannot compete with Edgartown — that stuffy place; even so, had the lady from Menemsha walked along William Street or viewed more closely some of the dwellings lining the harbor, she would have discovered houses of splendid symmetry and grace. She would have also found some of the noblest trees lining the streets of any town of its size on the Eastern Seaboard. It is this loose, amorphous "small townness" that so deeply appeals to me. A large part of the year I live in a rural area of New England where one must drive for miles to buy a newspaper. The moors of Chilmark and the lush fens of Middle Road then, despite their immense loveliness, do not lure me the way Vineyard Haven does. I like the small-town

Vineyard Haven Harbor taken from Owen Park

sidewalks and the kids on bikes and the trespassing gangs of dogs and the morning walk to the post office past the Café du Port, with its warm smell of pastry and coffee. I like the whole barefoot, chattering melee of Main Street — even, God help me, the gawking tourists with their Instamatics and their avoirdupois. I like the preposterous gingerbread bank and the local lady shoppers with their Down East accents, discussing *bahgins*.

Mostly I love the soft collision here of harbor and shore, the subtly haunting briny quality that all small towns have when they are situated on the sea. It is often manifested simply in the *sounds* of the place — sounds unknown to forlorn inland municipalities; even West Tisbury. To the stranger these sounds might appear distracting, but as a

fussy, easily distracted person who has written three large books within earshot of these sounds, I can affirm that they do not annoy at all. Indeed, they lull the mind and soul, these vagrant noises: the blast of the ferry horn — distant, melancholy — and the gentle thrumming of the ferry itself outward bound past the breakwater; the sizzling sound of sailboat hulls as they shear the waves; the luffing of sails and the muffled boom of the yacht club's gun; the eerie wail of the breakwater siren in dense fog; the squabble and cry of gulls. And at night to fall gently asleep to the far-off moaning of the West Chop foghorn. And deep silence save for the faint *chink-chinking* of halyards against a single mast somewhere in the harbor's darkness. Vineyard Haven. Sleep. Bliss.

William Styron and family

William Styron is the author of Sophie's Choice, *the much-lauded novel published in 1979 by Random House. His other works include* Lie Down in Darkness, Set This House on Fire, The Long March, *and the Pulitzer Prize-winning novel* The Confessions of Nat Turner. *He has also written a play,* In the Clap Shack *and numerous articles for a variety of magazines and journals. Born in Newport News, Virginia, and a veteran of the Marine Corps, and a graduate of Duke University, Mr. Styron still retains a southern style.*

CHAPPAQUIDDICK
Vance Packard

A **t the moment** Chappaquiddick Island is a state of mind, not an island. We are in a phase where an opening at the bottom of Katama Bay has sealed shut. This has happened periodically in recorded history. We are linked to the Vineyard mainland by a three-mile spit of sand. Most of us hope the linkage is temporary.

I look at this spit resentfully as I type this. We will probably remain tied to the mainland until another hurricane blasts open a new opening. We know where the opening will appear. It will be near the mainland, because the offshore water is deepest there. This permits a bigger bang. Then the opening will work its way eastward toward Chappy about 250 yards a year until after about 20 years the opening will reach Chappaquiddick and seal up.

Chappaquiddick is wildly irregular in shape but about three miles wide at its widest and about five miles long at its longest. Almost the entire island is surrounded by magnificent sand beaches. East Beach, where Senator Edward Kennedy was headed the night he went off the bridge, is probably the most splendid stretch of unspoiled beach left in North America. It stretches for five miles from the lighthouse on the north to Wasque Point on the south. The turbulent water off Wasque is famed as a fishing ground for the fighting blues, often running up to 16 pounds.

Most of Chappaquiddick is covered with dense woodland: scrub pine and oak. Near the shore there is much sea grass, wild grapes, beach plums, blueberries, wild roses. A few dozen deer roam the interior. The alarmed flutter of ring-necked pheasants is a common sound. Along the beaches, in addition to the gulls and terns, are egrets, yellowlegs, and great blue herons. In the fall the waters fill with squadrons of diving ducks.

While some hills rise nearly a hundred feet, the so-called topsoil is mostly sand. Chappaquiddick is quite young geologically, a remnant of the last retreating Ice Age. The southernmost mile of the island consists of moors so lovely that a decade ago when developers began eyeing it local residents spent a few hundred thousand dollars to make it into a wildlife reservation. Much of East Beach from the lighthouse down also has protected reservation status.

As for human habitat, there are now a couple hundred houses. Except for the Point area at the far north where the ferry makes its hundred-yard run to Edgartown proper, Chappy is lightly settled, with a dozen year-round families.

One brake on development is that in some areas

Cape Poge Lighthouse

*Aerial view of Katama Beach, showing a temporary opening
which separates Chappaquiddick from the rest of the Vineyard*

it is hard to get a clear title. In the early part of the century developers drew up designs for "cities" complete with boulevards and bandstands on Chappy and sold off lots by mail order. I talked once with a waitress in Brockton, Massachusetts, who mentioned that she owned a little plot of land somewhere on Chappy. She didn't know where.

And then there are the Indians looming in the background to inhibit land sales, particularly on North Neck. Up until 1900, much of the island was accepted as Indian land. Some Bostonian

professing Indian blood recently brought suit to reclaim a few valuable acres of shorefront. This past summer I was conducting interviews with longtime residents to help develop an oral history of the island. One respondent recalled seeing wigwams in a certain area. His wife reprimanded him and asked me to delete the details from the tape.

Another inhibition on heavy development is that most of the land with water view is controlled by families who have lived on the island at least

Dyke Bridge

Dune grass protects the eastern ridge of Chappy.

The Chappaquiddick ferry in action

a quarter of a century, or have relatives who did. Many families with different names have interconnections through blood ties. And most of these families are passionately isolationist and want to keep the island the way "it was," even if this may mean enduring dirt roads, and poor ferry service off season.

Newcomers to Chappy frequently ask the obvious question: Why don't they build a bridge to connect Chappaquiddick to the mainland of Martha's Vineyard? It would require no major engineering feat. Designs for such a bridge were drawn up by engineers at least fifty years ago. But people asking the question about a bridge are given a chilly treatment. No one that I know of wants a bridge.

One of America's most eminent social commentators, Vance Packard lives part of each year on Chappaquiddick, in a sprawling beach house. He is the author of such books as A Nation of Strangers, The Status Seekers, The Hidden Persuaders, *and most recently,* The People Shapers. *While on the Vineyard, Mr. Packard spends much of his time swimming in the inlet that borders his home, or fishing off the dock. Aside from the Island, he spends the fall and spring in New Canaan, Connecticut, and the winter in Mexico. It's a hard life.*

THE VINEYARD'S GRAPES OF WRATH

John B. Oakes

Martha's Vineyard is not merely one more of the hundreds of pleasant islands lying off the New England coast for the delectation of summer visitors. Nor is it a museum piece. It is, rather, a living organism, a viable community of more than eight thousand permanent residents whose roots go back to the earliest days of European settlement in America. It embraces an extraordinary complex of resources, both man-made and natural.

The thick oak woods and teeming marshes, the uplands and sweeping moors, the dunes and ponds punctuated by towering coastal cliffs and ringed by gentle beaches constitute as variegated a landscape in the small space of a hundred square miles as can be found on the Eastern Seaboard — all surrounded by relatively warm waters as notable for their fishing resources as for their recreational quality.

The geology of this island is alone enough to give Martha's Vineyard a special scientific distinction, augmented biologically by the abundance and variety of its bird life and botanically by the wide range of its plant life. Its permanent population, largely of Yankee and Portuguese descent, includes the remnant of an Indian tribe, while the island is also notable for the long-existing comity here of blacks and whites — probably the oldest major vacation spot in the United States where blacks have formed so significant a part of the resort community. The whaling captains' mansions at Edgartown, the Camp Grounds at Oak Bluffs, the 18th- and 19th-century farmhouses still scattered about the island add to its architectural and historic interest as they bring the past vividly into the present. Martha's Vineyard forms a stable, ecological whole whose delicately adjusted mechanism for growth can be — and is being — ruptured through a false sense of security, indifference, and simple greed.

It was in the early 1960s that developmental pressures stimulated by an increasingly affluent mainland society began to be felt on the island. "The blight of unbridled subdivision and the inroads of tasteless commercial exploitation are only just beginning on Martha's Vineyard," reported one observer in October 1964. "Of particular concern is the fact that the island is absolutely unprotected against exploitation." And for the next several years it remained virtually unprotected, while the opportunities to prevent inroads into particularly fragile areas diminished day by day.

*The unspoiled beauty
of the South Shore still remains.*

What was happening to the coastal zone throughout America during these years ought to have been of sufficient warning to the Vineyard. Two major presidential reports in the sixties urged national action to save the disappearing shoreline as a national resource; in 1970 the Interior Department put forward an imaginative proposal to shield the most vulnerable of America's islands, specifically including the Vineyard, from the haphazard and frenetic exploitation that was already threatening most of them.

This was the aim, too, of Senator Kennedy's bill, introduced in 1972, to establish a sensible pattern of land use for the Vineyard with the aid of federal funds, allowing for orderly, locally approved development in those areas best able to absorb it, while protecting those that weren't. The Islanders' inherent mistrust of federal intrusion was typically

exploited by real-estate, construction, hotel, and commercial interests opposed for obvious reasons to every form of land-use control. The result was that the Kennedy bill was eventually shunted aside — and with it the best chance of preserving those values of the Vineyard that were in the most immediate danger.

Meanwhile, the Martha's Vineyard Commission, a weakly structured planning body set up under state law in a successful effort to deflect support from the Kennedy bill, has been so severely crippled already by withdrawal of two of the Island's six towns from its jurisdiction that even this feeble attempt to set guidelines for the Vineyard's growth may flounder altogether. If it does, the Vineyard will be opening itself to a period of virtually unchecked pressures that will impose intolerable economic and physical strain on the Island and its facilities while undermining the quality of Island life in the process.

Despite such warning signals as the urban sprawl already creeping out from its main centers of population, Martha's Vineyard is still relatively intact. But it will not be for long. To quote a recent headline in the *Gazette:* "Edgartown Building Slump Turns into Boom Again." Plans for subdivisions are popping out all over. It is estimated conservatively that some five thousand additional homes — most of them "second homes" — may be built on the Island within the next decade, bringing in their train additional urban

*Pristine winterscape
in Chilmark*

Nature's damage to a Menemsha wharf

traffic jams, shopping centers in rural areas, wide-shouldered thoroughfares bearing no relation to the land, and lowering of water tables and of water quality — in fact, the suburbanization of the entire Island, to the immediate profit of a few and the permanent spiritual and economic impoverishment of all.

Coming events cast their shadows before. All we have to do is look at Route 28 from Wareham to Buzzard's Bay, and along the South Shore of Cape Cod. It could happen here; and unless we become more sensitive to the intangible values of this island than we have been in the past, and act accordingly — it surely will.

Beach road bumbaclaat, August

John B. Oakes, the former editor of the editorial page for The New York Times, *has been a summer resident of Chilmark since 1962, and an active conservationist since the 1930s. His byline appears frequently on the Op-ed page of the* Times.

A MIGHTY ANGLER BEFORE THE LORD

Red Smith

"**G**randpa," the fisherman said, watching his companion crawl under a barbed-wire fence, "did you grow old or were you made old?"

The fisherman had a little plastic rod and a spinning reel with a bobber on the line. He had dug worms out of a compost heap and now he dunked one in Turtle Pond on Ozzie Fischer's farm near Beetlebung Corner. He watched the bobber intently, moving his bait here and there beside lily pads. White water lilies rested on the surface, their petals opened fully. Water striders darted about in cheeky defiance of natural laws. The fisherman noted a wooden structure floating in the middle of the pond.

"The dog has to swim to his house," he said.

"It does look like a dog house," he was told, "but Mr. Fischer built that for ducks in case they wanted to make a nest in it and lay their eggs."

Not even a turtle showed interest in the worm. This may explain why you never see anybody fishing Turtle Pond. However, the swan pond in West Tisbury was only a fifteen-minute drive down Island, and it is common to see boys fishing there. Probably the proper name is Mill Pond, but in the fisherman's family it is known as the swan pond because a cob and his pen live and love and rear their cygnets there.

The fisherman was thoughtful on the drive. "Do people who don't have a birthday grow older?" he asked.

Yes, he was told, there is one way to avoid that, but the method isn't recommended.

"Some people don't have a birthday," he said. "They have to pick July." After a silence he added an afterthought. "Or December. I'd pick July."

"It's August now," he was reminded.

"Yes, but there'll be another July."

"Oh you mean next July. Yes, there are always two — last July and next July." He thought that over and smiled as if the idea pleased him, but he made no comment.

The swans were at the far end of their pond. On

The fishin' hole, West Tisbury

the water beside the road were a dozen or more mallards. Parking, the fisherman's companion asked: "How old are you now?"

At first there was no answer. Then, tentatively: "Six."

"Oh? When will you be six?"

"Tomorrow." His birthday is in September.

Reddish-brown weeds showed a little below the surface. "Throw it where the ducks are," the fisherman said. He laughed when the bobber, split shot, and hook plopped in near a duck, startling her.

"Now hold the rod still and watch the bobber," he was told.

"What's a bobber?"

"That red-and-white thing."

"That's a floater," he said, but not impatiently.

Drawn by curiosity, two ducks swam slowly toward the bobber, eyeing it.

"I have to go to the bathroom," the fisherman said. He saw some tall shrubs. "I'll go behind there." He went off at a trot.

While he was gone the bobber submerged but the bait was lifted clear before a fish could strip the hook or, worse, get himself caught in the fisherman's absence.

"A fish pulled the floater under water," he was told on his return. "Be ready to catch him."

In a few moments the bobber broke into a jig. The fisherman cranked his little tin reel. Except for a tiny nubbin of worm, the hook was bare.

"The worms are in the car," his companion said.

"Keep fishing with that and I'll get another." By the time he got back the hook was clean.

"Next time the floater sinks," it was suggested, "jerk your rod up first to set the hook in the fish and then crank." In a moment: "There! Good, now crank. No, I'm afraid you're caught in the weeds. Just keep cranking. No! You have a fish. Keep cranking. See him?"

A pale belly flashed right, left, and right again. His lips set, the fisherman reeled furiously. He dragged a nine-inch bullhead onto the bank and stared at it.

"Is that the first fish you ever caught?"

"Yes." The tone was hushed.

"Come on, then. We'll take it home and I'll skin it so your mother can cook it."

"My mommy will laugh her head off," he said. He was jubilant now. "I'm crazy about my family," he said. "My mother and father and my sister and my cousin Kim, they'll laugh their heads off."

Red Smith's regular sports column for The New York Times *(and before that,* The New York Herald Tribune *for twenty-one years) has become a staple for all well-informed, sophisticated fans. He covers the full spectrum, from baseball to hockey. He now lives in Chilmark in a tasteful home in the woods and is married indeed. His favorite sporting event on the Vineyard is the annual horse pull at the Agricultural Fair.*

Chilmark schoolchildren learning softball during morning recess, dreaming of the day they'll be old enough to join The Sunday Game.

THE GOINGS-ON IN MURIEL TOOMEY'S BACK LOT

Robert Crichton

You wouldn't notice it, not unless you were specifically searching it out. Some people I know who have spent each summer for the past twenty years on the Vineyard, in Chilmark, passing it every Sunday morning, have never noticed it or suspected its existence.

There's no attempt to hide it, to keep it a private affair. A white, running down, onetime farmhouse shields it a little from the road, and a scattering of wind-whipped pines cuts the view, but it's there to be seen. It's just that, as with so many things on the Vineyard, it doesn't draw attention to itself and makes no effort to draw any. But in this town of Chilmark, past Beetlebung Corner on the road that runs out to Gay Head, just south of that road looking toward the sea, in Muriel Toomey's back lot — every seasonable spring and summer Sunday — they have been playing a baseball — softball, now, as the generations become — well, softer — game for the past fifty-three years. Longer, some say, much longer, but the consensus is that the game began in 1926.

What is remarkable about this game is not the game itself; this it is not, but the circumstances surrounding it — the rules and codes and traditions that have grown up to meet new needs and stayed the same to satisfy old ones, with no rules committee needed, no speeches made, nothing ever written down, to become a Chilmark tradition, one very special to this place. The basic rule has always been simple: What's best is what's right and what's right is what works best, no matter what the rule book says — Yankee pragmatism in its finest low-keyed flowering.

Camus would have approved of the Chilmark ball game — no hard, abstract set of rights and wrongs but only the consequences of acts. The game is all of that — the consequences of fifty-three years of common sense, dealt out with an easygoing generosity of spirit all directed to one end: having fun, despite the great coach Vince Lombardi roaring down from heaven that no, winning is all that counts, is what the game is all about. All about in Chilmark, that is, not that they don't play to win.

A LITTLE HISTORY

At the start the game was a family affair, fathers and sons, big brothers and little brothers, a few daughters, and some, to this day, regret the passing of this gentler game. Some went away from it and never came back. But the fact was that, as a game, it didn't work. No grown-up can guarantee that a ball he hits will not bounce up and deliver a hefty whack to some ten-year-old, perhaps ruining the game for him forever. There is no history on this but I am forced to deduce that after the third or fourth youngster was carried home with a knot on his head the children began to sit on the sidelines, as they do today, and cheer on their fathers and big brothers.

Women's liberation and baseball in the laissez-faire, let-it-be tradition of the Vineyard, a tradition that grows as you move up-Island, came early. Married women, mothers, and young women showed up at Toomey's lot and were accepted in. This open-minded approach persisted for many years, but — counter to the national trend, the Vineyard always out of step with the nation somehow — dwindled away for the old classic reason: It didn't really work.

One of the not very subtle secrets about baseball is that there lurks, in every player, some driving primal lust to belt a ball as hard and true as a person can bring wood to leather. There are few more satisfying sensations in sports than knowing, on the moment of impact, that you have, by God, met the ball *right,* and then to witness the end result of that rightness arch up and away — white against the sky, on the Vineyard whiter yet against a sea-scraped sky.

The Great Women's Dilemma, which led to a female boycott and the forming of a woman's game, was that few women could hit a ball all that hard. Men played close in and gobbled up slow rollers, making it no contest. Later a code was established, named the Connecticut Rule — by me, I think, because I learned it there — that all players must play back at normal depth, causing many balls — little squibbers and nudgers — to be turned into hits just because they were so badly hit. This wasn't satisfying to anyone, and the women began to drift out of the game. A few intrepid women still show up and play, they are still welcome, and I have no doubt that eventually there is going to emerge in Chilmark a woman who will be able to strike out her husband four times in a game, thereby ruining his week and possibly his marriage as well.

THE FIELD

Mrs. Toomey's field is one of the worst fields to play softball on in the United States. I know one worse, in a coal town in West Virginia where the fielders have to take their shoes off, and ford a rushing mountain stream, to reach the outfield. There is nothing that can be done about this except re-create the state. There is plenty that could be done to Toomey's lot, which is why it is so uniquely Vineyard. In fifty-three years nothing has ever been done.

In any other town a grounds committee would be formed and some gravel-voiced leader would have

The action is fierce at the Sunday game.

men and boys out with shovels and rakes and mowers Getting the Field Ready. This was once actually suggested in Chilmark. It was highly approved of but no one ever showed up. As the Algerians used to say, "We have learned to live with our war." Chilmark ballplayers have learned to live with theirs.

The foul lines are incorrect. They have always been incorrect. But everyone knows *how* they are incorrect, so that a ball landing fair to the outsider's eye is mysteriously foul, and certain foul balls — foul in Iowa or Texas — for reasons impossible to describe, are as true and good in Chilmark as Swiss francs.

The pitching mound is 2½ feet too close to the plate. All pitchers are allowed to pitch illegally from it. Reason: If they pitched legally on that field no one would ever get put out. What is illegal in the rest of the world is legal here because it works better. An outsider once said: "That isn't a legal pitch. You're doing it all wrong here." It is said that no one ever spoke to him again. He summers in New Jersey now.

Such deep holes have been gouged out in the "batter's box" that small players offer almost no strike zone to pitch to; they are knee deep in the Vineyard.

Let us dispose of the outfield quickly. Right field goes uphill through a potholed pasture, levels out on a fairly well-traveled road, and then leaps up onto the poison-ivy-clustered lawn of some

immensely generous people who have had Sunday brunch after brunch disrupted by balls cascading off their picture window and outfielders shouting down that they are not going to look for the ball in that ivy. No one, yet, has ever been run down on the road.

In center field there are two hazards to try men's souls. One is a long and gentle dip, and many an outfielder, fleetly floating down the dip, has suddenly found his legs disappearing from under him. Some of the crashes have been quite spectacular. In deep dead center the dip is more meaningful. Here is one of the pots left behind in the Vineyard's terminal moraine when the great glacier melted. Into this fielders don't dip, they drop and disappear, sometimes not to be seen soon again. On an island where men went out in boats far smaller than that sink hole after whales far larger it seems fitting that the first question asked is not "Is he alive?" but "Did he hang onto the ball?"

Left field is a delusion. It entices and a little knoll in deep left invites the idea that a long ball up on that knoll will be an automatic home run when, in fact, it is an automatic out for any decent fielder and as such is known as "The Graveyard." Just over the knoll, however, lies a clutch of pine trees, and a ball knocked into them is often a home run. There is the old World War I poem:

> In Flanders fields the poppies blow
> Between the crosses row on row

David Flanders, the up-Island real-estate baron, hit so many balls into those pines that the poem has been restated:

> In Flanders fields the softballs go
> Among the pine trees row on row

It *is* Toomey's lot but for those with a memory of those towering drives this small section forever Flanders fields shall be.

The basepaths are hard to describe, but self-respecting cattle have been seen avoiding them. The bases are often anything that comes to hand. I once slid into second and the base was a copy of Joyce's *Portrait of the Artist as a Young Man.* That I call Chilmark class. Anyone who slides in this game should really be checked out at Austin Riggs or flown down to Bellevue for heavier treatment, but slide they do. When you notice young men in Chilmark with their jeans ripped to shreds the chances are that they are not being Edgartown hip but that they have — simply — slid for home on Toomey's lot.

THE UMPIRES

No one knows where they come from or who appoints them, they simply are umpires: men of authority, noble age, and, sometimes, failing

David Flanders points to his pine lot.

Lenny Dourmashkin, resident umpire

eyesight. The loudest and most indomitable of them all was Roger Baldwin, the founder of the American Civil Liberties Union and now in his nineties. He never called a wrong play. He told me that. When one umpire retires, another one, no one knows how, appears next week as if designated by the Deity. In my time perhaps the most notable was Rabbi David Wice of Philadelphia.

"Not only am I umpire here and as such always right, I also have God on my side."

Very hard to argue with. The rabbi evidently had some optical disorder causing him to see balls that sailed a good foot over the batter's head as cutting the heart of the plate. This was all right for Chilmark; the rabbi called them the same way for both sides. God is fair. What you did was learn to live with it. When a ball came in at head level, you swung. This was known as a Rabbi Wice strike. House guests would ask me: Why did you swing at a ball up there, for God's sake?

Because it was right over the heart of the plate, I would say, and everyone would nod. Very mysterious to outsiders.

Dr. Dourmashkin, who took over after Wice, was an excellent umpire, but he presented one special problem. He had three boys and, for a time, one daughter playing. They were among the better players ever to perform in Chilmark, but it did strike

people as odd that in five years, meaning in hundreds of games and thousands of times at bat, no Dourmashkin was ever known to go down on strikes. How the good doctor loved those boys. Chilmark solution to balance it out: Never allow two Dourmashkins on the same team at the same time.

THE PLAYERS

The game, in theory and for a long time in fact, was to start at ten o'clock sharp. The idea behind this was that everyone, even the slugabeds, could be assembled, and the players for the first game of the morning — the elite game — would be picked. Elite because the twenty best players in Chilmark would, naturally, be the first picked from what is known as the Slave Market.

The Slave Market is just what it sounds like. All the potential and hopeful players line up trying to look nonchalant and as if they couldn't care less whether they got chosen or not and then, by some sort of haphazard but mutually understood way, two of the better players — ideally the two best pitchers for balance — are designated to begin picking a team — separating the wheat from the chaff. As each man is picked they gather around their captain, look up and down the shuffling line, and summon the next man out of line.

This can be tense and revealing. You are on the

Open picking at the Slave Market

line. You are being publicly weighed and judged by your peers. For young players it can be exciting because being picked for the first game is their certification that they have finally made it. For the older players, being passed over after years of being picked for the first game can be a little painful.

But this doesn't last long. The team that wins the first game — thereafter known as the Clam Diggers — gets to stay on the field, and a new team is summoned from the Slave Market, and another team after that one. Everyone — bum or Babe — except for rare occasions when too many show up, is entitled to play. Today the first game tends to start as soon twenty players arrive on Toomey's lot. This may cut down on elitism but it also cuts down on the drama of the choice and balance. When you choose from forty or so men, you tend to field two teams remarkably similar in talent and this makes for close, tight games.

As far as talent goes, the level is deceptively high. Because of the field and the clothes the players wear, they don't look very good until the experienced eye discovers, behind those scruffy façades, some very capable ballplayers. Perhaps the most consistently effective player for many years was David Flanders, aptly known, out of his hearing, as the Chilmark Whale. For years Flanders was first chosen. For years no one hit a ball farther or harder, up into his beloved patch of pines. Then age began to take its toll and the ball began to fall just a little short of the pines into the waiting glove of a fielder in the Graveyard. And then Malcolm came to town. No one knew much about Malcolm, he looked like Central Casting for Billy Budd. He

played, I think, about eight games, and during that time hit about twenty balls so far out that at least ten of them were never found again. He went away as quietly as he came, and most people were secretly glad Malcolm went. For one thing, we were running out of balls. But rumor has it he will return next summer.

A very strange thing happened the winter after Malcolm. Someone, in the dead of night and in the dead of winter, with terrific effort, moved the pine trees. That next spring the trees were ten or twelve feet closer to home plate. No one knows who did it, although rumor and innuendo about the mystery of the moving pines has never totally ceased.

Consistently the worst-*looking* player is the editor of this book, Peter Simon. There is nothing outwardly about Simon to inspire confidence. He cannot possibly throw a ball the way he throws it, but the ball gets there. He surely can't hit the way he holds the bat, but hit it he does; one of the most consistently reliable hitters in Chilmark for a good many years. Which brings me to the most revealing and, I suppose, meaningful point to this Chilmark tale.

In over thirty-five years of playing in games like this — on Long Island, Connecticut, Cape Cod, and so on — players like Peter and men as old as me would never be picked to play. In all of those places there grew up a controlling clique who dominated the game and who got to play in it. Outsiders need not apply.

What is conspicuous in Chilmark is the absence of cliques. No tight little in-bunch that each week makes a deal to pick each other and keep the game to themselves. What is conspicuous is a respect for the individual person, and the source of that is simple generosity. The rule governing the marathon Chilmark game — and I use the game now as a metaphor for the Island as a whole — is tolerance.

When I first showed up to play I hid my mitt because, if I was denied admission to the game, which I suspected I would be, I didn't want to look foolish and rejected. I took my chance but I figured the local boys, the Islanders, would have their game locked up with an outsider getting to play when someone got hurt or had to go harpoon a swordfish.

But when I got to Toomey's lot I couldn't tell who were the natives and who were the off-Islanders, except for a few psychiatrists. I could tell by his accent that one of the men picking up a team certainly wasn't born and raised where there was sea and sand. I had never seen that before, the natives and the summer people, working things out right, in an easy, relaxed, unself-conscious way. Rich and powerful men have played in these games. No one ever knew, or if they knew, cared. Once I couldn't resist telling someone who a famous, one-game visitor was.

"Well, he sure is a lousy second baseman," was the response. So much for fame. The only person I recall making any waves at all and then not very much — and that I'm afraid of my doing — was the great baseball player Jackie Robinson. In the ninth inning with men on base I stepped back from the plate:

"Now batting for Crichton, Jack R. Robinson," and handed him my bat. He fondled the bat and peered out at the pitcher. He clearly wanted to give it a try but then he handed the bat back. What I remember is the silence of respect that no one else was ever accorded on that field.

"No, you'll do better than me."

We didn't know he was almost blind then. He died a few weeks later.

The point the game makes is that, unlike every resort I at least have been to, is how little snobbishness there exists here, and how little resentfulness. There's no base for it. No starting point for it. No clubs to exclude anyone from. You can't socially scare anyone when there isn't too much to exclude people from. There is the same sun and sand and sea and sky and the same fish to be caught. If you want that social thing you quickly learn you came to the wrong place.

"Why, this place is a social desert," I heard someone describe Chilmark.

How fine, I thought. It really doesn't matter if your family came here three hundred years ago and it really doesn't matter if your family makes three hundred thousand dollars a year. It helps, of course, it alters things in some ways, like having a better mitt helps a little but not much in the long run.

You are what you are and what you bring with you. A man *is* a man for all that and all that, as Robbie Burns discovered so long ago.

If you want to see that played out before you, the truth of it in action, you might take a look at the goings-on in Mrs. Toomey's back lot.

Aside from playing softball, Robert Crichton writes epic novels from his home on the West Side of New York City. His books include The Great Impostor *and* The Secret of Santa Vittoria, *and he is trying to finish* Memoirs of a Bad Soldier. *He came to the Vineyard when a friend summered in Lobsterville. He said one day he just* had *to live in Lobsterville, but never did. Instead, Bob landed up in Chilmark off Middle Road. He took up playing ball to escape having to go into the ocean, which scared him.*

The Chilmark team photo, circa '77

Winter walk along Stonewall Beach

THE VINEYARD: A MODERN LOVE AFFAIR
Peter Barry Chowka

I came to the Vineyard for the first time in the early 1970s, by accident, almost, for what I thought would be a two-day visit. Overnight the Island seduced and won me. I ended up staying for three weeks and moved here from the city shortly afterward. Ever since then I have considered the Vineyard my home — it seemed unthinkable not to.

For a child of the suburbs, living on the Island provides a rich texture (where previously there had been only the coarse grain of modern conformity), a real sense of being grounded in a remarkable place, and a much-needed frame of reference for measuring the value of other places old and new. I have found none other to surpass or equal it.

My first Island winter, lonely in some ways, overall was an unceasing delight in finally finding a place where, as Henry Beston wrote a half-century ago of his beloved Cape Cod, "there always was something to do, something to observe, something to record, something to study, something to put aside in the corner of the mind."

Then, however long it sometimes seems, a winter on the Vineyard soon enough brings one face to face with the approach of summer and mixed feelings at the prospect of another "season." On one hand, the summer climate soothes and caresses luxuriantly; on the other, there is the onslaught of excesses and imbalances that result from the fragile economy's unhealthy overreliance on seasonal tourism to sustain itself. The differences are profound. In winter: isolation; too few people and activities; the precious ability, though, to enjoy unhindered almost any spot of one's choosing. In summer: suddenly most beaches off-limits to wanderers; "No Trespassing" signs enforced; in the towns a deluge of tourists and day-trippers and their by-products of traffic, crowding, tour buses, and noise.

As one of a steady stream who came spontaneously and stayed on, I see how it is possible to fit neither of the two dominant categories of modern Vineyard residents: native-born or regular seasonal visitor. Some residents are unable to relate to newcomers who are not summer people (economically necessary) or born here (automatically accepted). One could perhaps understand this curious attitude more easily if it included also a meaningful wariness of *things* not indigenous, like tract housing developments whose vacant ugliness looms during the off-season and the tacky, fast-buck hucksterism that definitively characterizes the summer.

The Island, of course, has attracted newcomers from the time of the first European settlers and, even earlier, the native Americans, led here, as legend goes, by the island-hopping giant Moshup. As usual, though, history tends to remember principally the exploits and accomplishments of those deemed noteworthy who left some sort of visible legacy: religious leaders, politicians, warriors, successful merchants, and whaling captains whose houses of residence and worship continue to stand as well-kept reminders of an earlier time.

Today the Vineyard has its summer celebrities and famous visitors who often overshadow its talented and interesting native or year-round people, and who gain for the place additional unnecessary national publicity. It is home, too, for many who choose to live quietly, eking out a living in a variety of unconventional, creative ways that span the spectrum of possibilities inherent in the term "voluntary simplicity."

A tiny microcosm of the whole complex American culture, the Island is home as well to many different viewpoints, *raisons d'être,* and lifestyles. I suspect that it has long been so — a magnet for original thinkers who have seen beyond their culture's headlong flight to progress, ease, and newness. There are ever more concrete indications of this flourishing diversity: the self-supporting guild of artists and craftspeople; the alternative food co-op; a vital and active antinuclear-power group; for a while during the midseventies a startlingly original FM radio station; writers and poets who crave the solitude; a small community of photographers dedicated to capturing the Island's special visual charm and sharing their images in the weekly *Gazette;* and people otherwise employed in a variety of gentle occupations.

These residents and their compatriots who visit from off-Island constitute a small, loose alternative network of sorts that coexists — as a vital underside — with the idealistic, mythical public-relations portrait of the Vineyard that persists in the Chamber of Commerce handouts.

Occasionally people come together — out of their woods, workshops, and studios — for communal events like the large, memorable antinuke concert-celebration in September 1978, the weekly visits to the co-op, or the meetings in late 1978 called to organize against another threatened intrusion of mainland consciousness — a national fast-food chain's design to establish an absurdly out-of-place franchise on Beach Road in Vineyard Haven.

Here many of us have decided to make our world, in field and forest, by seashore and pond, on hill and in valley — at the *place* where we actually live. Seldom is it essential to look much beyond. For those of us, like Beston, born in a "world sick to its thin blood for lack of elemental things," the simple elements that the Vineyard continues to offer are more than enough.

It is nothing less than a love affair that draws us and keeps us here. Unlike most other relationships today, it shows no signs of coming to an end.

Peter Barry Chowka gained a certain degree of Island notoriety when he led the successful campaign to "sack the Big Mac" in the fall of 1978. His other achievements include authoring extensive investigative reports on the politics of medicine, environmental cancer, and media manipulation, and interviewing a variety of cultural and political figures. He lives quietly down a small lane off Lambert's Cove Road where he is always busy, producing radio commentaries, writing various exposés for New Age *and other alternative-culture magazines, and watching "The CBS Evening News."*

"Sack the Mac" protesters show their enthusiasm by waiting in the rain outside a crowded Board of Health meeting in Vineyard Haven. They were pleased with the outcome.

*Part of the large audience at the "No Nukes" concert
held in Chilmark, September 1978. A memorable day for all*

*A display of
local issues*

A TREE GROWS IN THE SAND

Nelson Bryant

Whipped by winds from every quarter, drenched with salt spray, twisted and gnarled by the constant play of elemental forces, the cedars of Cape Poge, deep-rooted in infertile sand, somehow survive.

In summer, visitors to this narrow band of barrier dunes that separates a bay from the ocean will find silent, breathless sandy hollows shimmering in the sun, places to sunbathe or to dream among the stunted trees, few of which are more than twice the height of a man.

In winter, when a northwest gale shrieks across the bay, piling whitecaps, eelgrass, codium, scallops, quahogs and other shells on the shore, and carrying the indescribable aroma of the salt flats when the tide is down, the first ranks of cedars shudder and reel. But beyond them, deeper in the grove, so dense and intricate is their design, no wind invades. Often the outer trees are killed, but their writhing sun-bleached forms stand for many years.

Chickadees and other songbirds hide in that sanctuary all winter, and deer are also frequent sojourners there.

Within that slender grove, no more than two hundred yards wide at any point and perhaps three-quarters of a mile long, there are a few tiny freshwater ponds. In early winter, before the truly bitter cold, black ducks often tarry there in stormy weather. They do not arrive, as is their habit, until nearly an hour after sunset, but if the sky is clear one can stand among the trees and watch them arrive, dark wings set and cupped for a quick descent. And even if the sky is black, one can often see the ghosts of birds, sometimes real, sometimes imagined, close overhead and hear the whispering of their wings. Later, when the little ponds freeze,

Canada geese

*Swallows take rest before continuing
south for winter.*

Beach tree, Cape Poge

Spring meltdown at Beetlebung corner

the ducks must seek whatever lee the grasses and reeds and channels of the salt marshes provide.

Not many nights ago, when the heavens burned with a holy light, each star and planet polished by a fierce wind, I stood among those trees and marveled at their strength, and beside me, defying adversity with equal tenacity, a scrub oak sprawled, branches crawling along the sand instead of reaching for the sky.

Watching the cedars' spires grow black against the sun's last, cold, lingering light, thoughts reaching behind and before, I was not alone, for all of you were there, boys and girls, men and women I have known and loved, lashed by storms but rooted in hope, and the place I stood became a great cathedral, its nave the soaring curve of space.

Nelson Bryant was born in New Jersey but raised on the Vineyard, arriving at the age of eight. After enlisting in the 82nd Airborne, where he served through three campaigns, including the drop at Normandy, he became managing editor of a New Hampshire daily newspaper for fifteen years. He later returned to the Island, where he built docks before joining The New York Times, *where he writes a column called "Wood, Field and Stream," many of them from his home in Edgartown. As an author, he has published* Fresh Air, Bright Water, *and* Wildfowler's World. *Although constantly hunting and fishing, his hobbies are gardening, cabinetmaking, and poetry. An enigmatic ex-paratrooper, he has the soul of a poet and a marksman's eye.*

*The battle between sea, sand, cliffs
and man continues.*

YOU CAN STILL CHOOSE FOR THE VINEYARD

Anne W. Simon

I used to believe that the Vineyard would never change. That was its magic, a sleeping beauty untouched by the world. Each year it looked the same at first glance from the ferry deck, the same as we drove up-Island, marveling again at the green arches over quiet roads, the familiar panorama — blue pond, strip of dunes, the open sea beyond. The Island smelled the same, felt the same; the summer unfolded as it always had.

Such magical consistency makes people happy. "The Vineyard is my *real* home," off-Islanders say, planting gardens, walking the land, staying the year round when they can, getting married and buried here, and their children after them. Islanders, except for the few intent on development, believe the magic too. They shrug off signs of change, fight their internecine battles with the same fierce loyalties as ever, are together with summer people in the firmly held forever-thus fantasy.

There seems no pressing reason to surrender this dream. The Vineyard's wild beauty and natural bounty are still in evidence; glacial boulders still punctuate the curving shore, twisted oaks and cedars edge salt meadows. There are still blackberries if you know where to find them, still enough shorebirds to watch, enough fish for sportsmen and the Menemsha fishing fleet to catch, still some shellfish buried in shallow-pond bottoms. There is still cool water, hot sand, scarlet autumn, crisp white winter, doorside lilacs blooming in the spring.

All this encourages the conviction that the island is a world apart, allowing casual dismissal of one small change or another as unimportant. In the early seventies I studied the Vineyard's changes and wrote down the findings, a fact-gatherer flying in the face of cherished fantasy. I then spent five years examining the whole East Coast, Florida to Maine, and discovered that no one part can be separate from the rest, that the entire coast, Vineyard included (if a year or so behind the mainland), is undergoing fast radical alteration, some of it irreversible. Mostly, the future of the whole coast preordains the Vineyard's future.

But Vineyard-minded people can affect what the Island will be to a degree. With our particular knowledge of this remarkable place, with insights that are ours alone, we can use our passion for the Island to shape its change.

If we dare to look around, look ahead, there is still time to have something to say about threats to this place. Must there be oil wells in Georges Bank, one of the world's most productive fishing grounds some one hundred miles off Nantucket? Do we approve the sewage outfall across Vineyard Sound, a floating nuclear plant in this area? What is our judgment of further development of the Island, penetration of its freshwater table, a bridge from Woods Hole? Experience elsewhere on the coast helps us decide.

New uses of the coast and vastly more use of it than ever before seriously affect its natural life-support functions. We interfere with its precise interlocking systems. The sand system keeps us from drowning by its defenses against the sea; for this it must be free to move, assemble where it will, eroding here, accreting there. We try to make it stand still, locking it into concrete, building groins to catch it, building hotels, motels, a house with a view, on its dunes and beaches. Its protection is quickly and dangerously diminishing. So, too, with the wetlands system where rivers meet the sea and marshes convert solar energy into food for marine life. Wetlands are a necessary environment for migrating birds, small mammals, most fish species. They are also valuable real estate on the shorefront-hungry market; more than half of U.S. wetlands have already been lost to development, and most remaining marshes and estuaries are increasingly polluted with every change of the tide.

The ocean surrounds continents with a darkening mirror of the new coast uses. We learn that it is not, as has been thought until now, a bottomless sink, uncorruptible. Microscopic plankton crowd its surface by the billions, ingest whatever is in the sea, feed the ocean population — five sixths of all life on this planet. In just a few years we have changed their diet; now it includes quantities of poisons, more untreated sewage than the ocean can dissolve, more and more petroleum hydrocarbons, some of which sink to form an oil bank that oozes its daily unhealthy contribution to the sea. All this enters the food chain by the plankton route and becomes available on our tables.

The lengendary Man from Mars would judge us suicidal. Why do we continue on a course that we know must bring us disaster?

There are reasons, even if not good ones. The requirements of a natural working coast do not fit the present insistence on growth and development. For the coast to become a locus for building, for energy, it must be transformed, and the price of this transformation is high indeed. We can see the conflict on the Vineyard, see it even more clearly on Georges Bank.

In this renowned spot, dozens of species spawn and billions of fish eggs float in the shallow waters, developing new generations. The United States has leased thousands of acres in this area to oil companies, to explore, develop, and produce whatever oil and gas may lie buried there. The choice between the continuance of the most ancient and productive fish habitat known and a few weeks' extra oil supply has now been made, an agony between spirit and pocketbook, and a measure of where we stand as educated coast dwellers.

Our very recent discovery, revealed by overuse, is that the coast, unlike any other part of the continent, is one indivisible system. All of its parts — water, sand, fish, birds — are constantly moving, intermingling; its thousands of beaches, bays, and marshes are all connected. What happens to one affects the rest. Knowing this, we can look ahead with a certainty we did not have before. We can construct two scenarios for what will happen to the coast before the turn of the century, perhaps in the next ten years. Or it could be by 1984, a symbolic year for predictions. To some extent at least the choice between these scenarios is ours.

SCENARIO ONE

1984 IF WE CONTINUE BUSINESS AS USUAL ON THE COAST

There are "Unsafe for Swimming" signs on our beaches. If the signs don't convince you, the stench of dead marine creatures will. Shorebirds, deprived of their habitats, are few, fish and shellfish species disappear; what remains is scarce on the market, the price escalated to caviar range. We have abandoned hope of getting rid of poisons in the water such as deadly Kepone, dumped into the James River, Virginia, where it lies on the bottom feeding young striped bass, or the carcinogenic PCBs in the Hudson. Since fish, as we know, migrate, they become not only expensive but also dangerous eating everywhere, and fishing is a declining business, a sad sport.

Privacy on the coast is a memory. Even the most privileged, with armed beach guards — the new status symbol — find their private sands overrun. In the seventies population growth is three times the national average; by 1984 coast population has doubled and beaches have diminished. Massive development to house the influx converts historic seaside towns, and the shore is strip-zoned for tourist attractions. There are more thruways along the coast, more bridges to islands. The view seaward, unfamiliar, is of oil-well derricks, floating nuclear plants and shore-front. There are man-made industrial islands for the neighbors that nobody wants, ceaseless traffic of oil tankers from the new East Coast wells to new mainland refineries.

By 1984 we have added huge quantities of oil to the ocean. There is no turning back from the new reality — marine life forever immersed in an oil bath.

Sand dune foliage at Lambert's Cove Beach

Its effects are better known than the terrible suspicions of the early seventies, when measurement of oil's action on living tissue was just beginning to be measured. A modest enough spill of No. 2 oil landed in Buzzards Bay; in 1978, oil still pools your footprints if you walk there at low tide, many areas have not recovered their full complement of animal species, many animals are not behaving normally. Young fiddler crabs do not survive in the marshes where a small concentration of oil is found six years postspill. The clam flats are still closed, clam tissues enfused with oil.

In the midseventies, another neighborhood spill — that of the *Argo Merchant* — poured eight million gallons of industrial oil on Nantucket shoals in the spawning season. Tiny oil droplets, said by oil companies to be totally dispersed, were seen by scientists to cling to delicate egg membranes, increasing mortality. If the egg survived, abnormalities multiplied. Some oil hydrocarbons are found to be carcinogenic as tumors and other malignancies appear in molluscs exposed to the new oil bath. Oil interferes with lobsters' direction-finding systems — their ability to locate food and mates. Severe oil stress causes them to leave their burrows; they lie in the mud on their backs, tails half curled, antennae limp. Since burrows are their best defense against predators, oil is deadly to lobsters, one way or another.

Elsewhere, failure to look ahead brings formidable disasters to the coast in 1984. The shore was overbuilt and left shorn of its protection in the seventies; during that same decade the hurricane cycle temporarily lapsed. In 1984 it returns, causing havoc, many times that of bad-winter storms that even today flood hotel lobbies, crumble sea walls, overturn houses on dunes. Further coast development creates a critical sand shortage, failure of wetland function — an unnatural nonworking coast. If it was unanimously agreed to "save" the Vineyard in 1984, these coast conditions

will severely curtail the degree of saving possible.

One more prediction: In 1984, the toy-pail-and-shovel business is on the way out. Children born in the eighties do not go to the beach. They grow up with a shore concept different from that of all generations of waders and castlebuilders before them. To them, the shore is a dangerous place.

SCENARIO TWO —
1984   IF WE REVOLUTIONIZE OUR USE OF THE COAST

Beaches are clean; water, although already irreversibly contaminated, is no worse than it is today. Some parts of the shore have "No Trespassing" signs intended to keep the coast wild, a guaranteed habitat for many species. Elsewhere we can use the coast for enjoyment. Here there are access roads and parking lots so that everyone can get to the shore, swim, picnic, walk, rest. No one drives over beaches or dunes, no one dumps garbage or waste in coastal waters, no one builds on the shore.

No one, in fact, owns it. The coast has been removed from the market by congressional action. It is now a national trust, a uniquely designed entity for a unique part of the continent. Everyone's motive, whether from the terror of having experienced coast chaos or from love for the viable shore or both, everyone wants to take care of the coast so that it can function as it once did,

The end of an era?

A delicate balance exists where Tisbury Great Pond meets the Atlantic.

protecting us, supplying us with food, inspiring us with its beauty. Some grandparents remember how it was in the good old days, prepollution, predestruction; children learn in school what the shore is for and how to take care of it. The new national policy that protects natural coast function in partnership with states and localities filters through the nation to endow every citizen with a share in the new caretaking. It has quick, salubrious results.

Many shore species survive the stress of the seventies to flourish with a healthy coast. Shorebirds revive, fish and shellfish are again edible, and there are enough of them to support a coast fishing business and bring fish prices — and 10 per cent of the world's protein — within reach of most people.

In this 1984 scenario, drilling for oil off the coast is outlawed. Transportation of oil is reduced to a minimum as we concentrate on new forms of energy, and what transportation there is is almost completely safe. Existing designs for safe tankers are standard practice, and only those ships that meet their rigid requirements are allowed on the sea. Fleet owners and oil men are somewhat less rich but, one might guess, they sleep better at night.

Growth moves inland, off the coast, off islands. We visit the shore but do not build on it. Instead sturdy mountains, fields, and valleys sprout

vacation homes, retirement homes, and condominiums, and court the tourist business. Prohibited from using coastal waters for industry, we use the technology invented in the seventies to substitute. We adapt refineries, factories, and power plants to inland, perhaps underground settings where they cannot harm the coast. The thousands of lawsuits hurled at town, state, and nation in the revolutionary uproar accompanying this new coastal use are beginning to recede as benefits appear.

Giving up one kind of profit on the coast for another — money for survival — seems less a deprivation than a privilege as the terror of the coastal crisis disappears and there is increasing confidence of a safer life ahead.

No Island Is an Island *(1973), Anne Simon's frank and impassioned description of the threatened despoliation of Martha's Vineyard helped galvanize the Island forces for preservation. Ms. Simon, who has lived thirty summers in a nineteenth-century Menemsha farmhouse that keeps watch on Vineyard Sound and the narrow bracelet of the Elizabeth Islands, addressed herself to the problems of the entire coast in* The Thin Edge *(1978).*

Windy Gates looking west

OFF-SEASON
Douglas Cabral

Summer ended this year on a rainy Sunday in mid-October. The season had closed more than a month before, and the interval, this year as every year, for the fewer and fewer left to enjoy it, was charmed.

From early September until the fall morning when the hard easterly drives raw cold and rain ashore to cloud even the last memory of the summer just ended, it is as if we were truants. Summer houses empty and facing their nearly priceless vistas with shuttered windows, barren porches where leaves are gathering, vacant lawns where grass thickens and browns. The sun is just as bright, the sky just as summery, but the beaches host only friends. There are shopkeepers who close up a couple of afternoons a week now, or are open just weekends, so there's time to tan.

In Edgartown especially those strolling patches of Lilly Pulitzer colors, vivid greens, blues, and pinks are gone, though Lilly's is having a sale and so is Robin Hood's Barn. Along the main streets there's a stocktaking — "How's the summer been?" "What's the fall look like?" — and more often than not sales were good, but not great, and more often than not the weather, which did its best, is to blame.

More interesting than the shopkeepers are the builders and caretakers. In summer they've worked nonstop because the customers were at their elbows, or they've not done much because the customers were here but didn't fancy all that banging and sawing during what was supposed to be a vacation. So the moment to get it all done has arrived, the people are gone, the weather's still fine, winter looms to furnish the urgency. But the hitch is: the derby. Fishing, soon gunning, an urge to take the day off, paint up the skiff for scalloping, take the boat for a sail, spend an afternoon at Zack's. Beyond it all it's the derby that keeps the contractors' pickups full of fishing tackle, not lumber. The blues-are-running syndrome strikes at midsummer, but the tide's running strong after Labor Day.

Outside my window the harbor empties by stages. By the day after Labor Day the marinas are abandoned. There are no visiting powerboats hunched in twos and threes, moored with string mazes, charcoal burners blazing. The sudden, final curtain on the marina season reminds one of that annual marvel of business realism: Giordano's Italian restaurant at the foot of Circuit Avenue. On the day after, the chairs are up on the tables, the help's gone back to college, and the owner's packing for Florida. End of season with a slam.

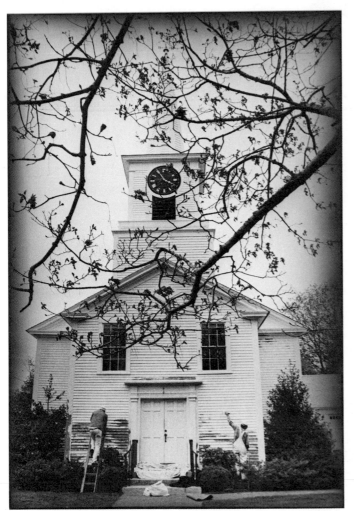

A change of season comes to the West Tisbury Congregational Church.

A good drying day, Vineyard Haven

The troops at Martha's Vineyard Shipyard, who've idled through the summer while the customers were off sailing, jump the gun to haul the boats whose masters have returned to the mainland. Soon, in the shortening daylight, the harder breezes of deepening autumn, only the diehard sailors go to sea. When October ends, of two hundred or so yachts moored at Vineyard Haven in July just six remain to face the winter's gales.

And beneath the still-bright days of dwindling summer is the vaguely unsettling knowledge that so many have left. Businessmen are off to big business elsewhere, students back to profound studies, journalists to city papers whose concerns are national, international, back to the world at large and its dimensions.

At the heart of deep winter on the Vineyard is the wind. The dependable southwester of summer keeps us cool — innkeepers advertise it, sailors swear by it. In winter the same southwester, and the warm rain it brings, is rare. The East, the rich fishy domain offshore, not frigid even in January, but always fierce, spawns the most dangerous gales, rain, or snow. The front face of my house, plainly

shingled, accustomed to the worst, faces directly east. The winter gale that comes overnight derides the furnace, freezes the front rooms, and the blast that flings seaweed over the brow of the beach into the pasture below the house, finds its way through storm windows and ancient sashes. The front door of one-and-one-quarter-inch-thick pine bows around the latch, snow shuffles into the hall under the weatherstripping.

In almost unbroken cycle, the easterly is followed by what the radio meteorologists call the "Arctic blast" or the "deep freeze" — a northwester, thirty-five to fifty knots of smartingly cold air. It freezes the moisture in the beach sand so footsteps leave no impression in the smoothed and furrowed surface off the shore. It keeps the furnace running without stop all night. Harbor ice, pond ice, even ice the reach of Vineyard Sound form in the face of the northwester.

On the morning of just such a northwest day the scallopers, very few of them, yellow sparks of color against the ruffled icy blue of Chilmark Pond, against the cloudless fierce blue of the sky, work anyway. In outboard motor-powered skiffs, in waterproof suits and rubber mittens they tow their drags and stand in the face of the wind picking over the debris for the

Bass Derby season

Scalloping on Sengekontacket

scallops. It is a livelihood when jobs are scarce, but it's a kind of myth too. Scalloping holds promise each fall of great windfalls for those few who stick it out. A good set of scallops means the three- or five-bushel limit can be had in two or three hours' work, and that means $75 to $125 for the scalloper. So the story goes. Reality rarely matches up, but in the down-Island towns, Edgartown especially, it comes respectably close.

Winter comes home to me in glimpses: from the road across the immense flat field, uncut corn stubble spiking through the snow, along whose west side the Seven Gates road winds; out along the wind-razed stretch of Dutcher Dock, nothing stirring, corn snow in caches here and there, against stacked lobster pots, laced over the heaps of scallop shells, spun over the marsh to the east; the clay cliffs from the beach below, rust and red and yellow against white, the scene of a horrible firefight, a bloodletting, the gray, miserable sea streaked and heaving below.

Whiling away the winter blues at the Chilmark store

Winter preparations begin in early fall, Gay Mark.

Winter's starkness at Quitsa Pond

Or at Oak Bluffs Harbor: the few small boats still at their moorings bearded with ice at the waterline and along the straining pennants; Fred Morgan's sleek commuter boat, used for his daily back and forth to Falmouth in all but the foulest weather; until February 1977 when it blew ashore, the *Tip Top,* Gerry Chipperfield's tired dragger, husky, formerly shapely, lately staying alongside a lot, too old to work safely in winter; Bruce Campbell's *Ranger,* Jim Lobdell's *Malabar,* Billy Austin's *Mary Eleanor,* Tony Higgins' *Nyatonga,* summer residents at Vineyard Haven Harbor sheltering for the bad months along the bulkhead in the lee of the East Chop Beach Club, sandblasted and leaping at their dock lines.

I think often of the February afternoon a year or so ago when I drove along the East Chop shore just after the blizzard and while the northwester screamed across the long fetch from the West Chop shore. I was out to see the gaiters, the mausoleums, the great coats and watch caps that the frozen spray sculpts around the spiles and timbers of the private docks that project from the beach in front of those precarious cottages. Two weeks of cold and northwest wind is sufficient to encase completely in ice the wooden framework.

That on the left, north. On the right, sheltered by the slim neck of sand, the glaze of asphalt, the homes on the brink and the boulders, now mammoth in their ice suits, placed to save the investment, is Crystal Lake. In outline much like the Vineyard itself, this shallow marsh-rimmed lake was frozen, mostly smooth, scoured of snow, and empty except for one man skating.

I had never thought about Dave Whittemore ice skating, but there he was spinning around the rim of the lake, cutting figures, an expert it appeared, absorbed, remembering, not stiffly but cautiously, the prowess of years. He was not smiling, and for a long time he did not catch sight of me. He whizzed and twirled, assumed the disciplined posture of the ice sprinter, one arm behind his back, the other pumping, he watched the ice, his feet, he clasped hands behind his back and meandered along. Dave Whittemore, sailor, fisherman, archer, businessman, cutting figures on Crystal Lake, the boarded windows of the summer homes looking on.

I think too of the moist, snowy, afternoon twilight of late December, the fields between the road and Fred Fisher's barn, the lights of the farm just a loom in the murk of the storm. One Christmas Eve Fred rented us his wagon for a hayride. We wanted to go out caroling. "Take the wagon," Fred said, "but I'm not going, no, sir." It was so cold as we raced over the Lagoon

Spring runoff at Gay Head Beach

Bridge there were no carolers visible under the hay and blankets when we got to the hospital. Fred knew better.

Winter is the time to stick by the stove, worrying whether the pipes will freeze, plowing out the road or staying in till someone does it for you, flying South in February to St. Thomas, Virgin Gorda, Key West, Nassau, anywhere warm. February is the cruelest test. It is also the end of the worst of winter.

Spring stutters and deepens through March, April, and May. Warm, magical days tempt gardeners to take off or turn in the seaweed blanket, and sailors to slip out in their tattered vessels once or twice before hauling them for the annual paint and putty work. And then it rains, coldly now where rain was a respite just a month or two ago. So much to do, and between

the rain and the garden and the boat and the urge to float through the finest spring days, so little time to do it all.

One still morning Joyce and I breakfasted with Yvette Eastman at her Gay Head hilltop home looking out over Menemsha Pond. The ground was cold but softening, unable any longer to resist the blandishments of the sun as it moved North. It was a Sunday, noiseless, not a car along the State Road all the way from Beetlebung Corner to Yvette's turnoff above Moshup Trail. At the table outside her front door we watched, stunned by the peace and the warmth.

Beyond the narrow neck at Quitsa and Stonewall ponds the South Shore stretched away in the morning blaze strait to Wasque. It was so far off, so much beyond the time and place, it was just exactly

Fred Fisher and his team, ready to roll

63

Getting the garden in

springtime, perceived as foreground and background, cool, warm, quiet, frantic, the end of one season — the beginning of another.

Fred Fisher helps mark this beginning by hitching his handsome stalwart pair to the plow instead of the hay wagon. Fred's thick round form shambles along as the horses march across the fields Fred owns along the State Road in West Tisbury. Fred is a man determined to do without illusions, to stare life's every smarting reality in the face, to say "just as I thought." And still spring finds him out behind his team, grumbling, plodding through the stirring, tumbling earth where he'll plant his corn.

Strange faces, almost familiar, almost forgotten pop out of doorways on Main Street. "How was the winter?" "Fine. When are you opening?" "Are you here for the summer already?" "No, just for the weekend."

"How was the winter?" she asked. Compared to what? I hadn't thought to measure it, except to remark that it included too many feet of snow, much too many buckets of rain, that it was terrifically busy, being cold and windy, lonely perhaps, very friendly on the other hand, and now it's spring. I hadn't thought to compare it to the other winters past, and certainly not to the summer ahead. But then springtime has come around, and it is nearly Memorial Day, and maybe the best answer is, "Too brief." But anyway, spring lingers.

Although the first great business weekend is Memorial Day, the season does not begin till July. There is time yet to enjoy the Vineyard as if it were the exclusive realm of those who spent the winter, as if the crowds of July and August will not come, never have, as if the still-empty summer homes are vestiges of a strangely unremembered seasonal population of years long gone now.

Douglas Cabral was managing editor of the Vineyard Gazette *from 1974 to 1979. During that era, he was solely responsible for all the lovely captions that accompanied* Gazette *photographs, which were also chosen by him. Before moving to the Vineyard in 1969, he worked as a free-lance writer for various boating publications, including* Soundings, National Fisherman, *and* Yachting. *He and his wife, Joyce (both are, coincidentally, from the town of Fairhaven, Massachusetts, about twenty miles inland from the Vineyard), live in a classic Cape house overlooking Vineyard Haven Harbor where Doug keeps the pulse of the Island.*

UP-ISLAND JOURNAL
Stephen Davis

May 28 It's the beginning of another summer, and time to reopen my squalid little hut on top of a petite hillock overlooking Menemsha Pond in Chilmark. Typically, we miss our four forty-five ferry reservation, racing up to the slip just as the crew pulled the chain over the last standby car to make it on the boat. We weep and plead to no avail, and are shunted to the end of the dreaded "guaranteed standby" line where we stew in our own juices for four hours until finally we inch forward onto the *Islander.* We overhear our fellow passengers complaining about the Vineyard. An Edgartown type uniformed in those hideous red flannel trousers and topsiders is earnestly lecturing his son that the Island is doomed. Another Ivy Leaguer, looking like a prep-school headmaster disguised as a lobsterman, laments that the "old Vineyard" is gone forever. A woman porting one of those damned Nantucket Lightship baskets is whining to her husband that she gives the Vineyard "twenty years at best before they build the bridge from Woods Hole." Amid these awful prophesies it occurs to me that Martha's Vineyard is still big enough to harbor some very different species. Imagine the difference between the stockbrokers and mortgage bankers in their manses on West Chop and Edgartown and the artists and writers tucked away off the road in their primitive hovels in Gay Head. Three summer months a year, Dukes County — the Vineyard and the Elizabeth Islands — is the richest in Massachusetts. For the other nine months, it's the poorest county in the state and the home of my particular friends, the Vineyard counterculture/Bohemia — carpenters, painters, poets, craftspeople, and fishermen who survive on the fringe of a fringe economy and live in voluntary poverty on perhaps the most beautiful landscape on the East Coast if not the planet. As the ferry docks and we drive through the suburban sprawl of Vineyard Haven, I realize I don't have much of an idea of what life is like in the down-Island towns. Only when I get past the Grange Hall in West Tisbury do I really feel I've arrived, up-Island, home again.

May 29 It's the usual opening-day scene at our hut. Rat excrement glows a bubonic green under the sink. Wide involuntary skylights in the ceiling. The bathroom floor rots away good-naturedly. We throw everything outside and attack with vacuum, broom, and paint to the best of our feeble ability without running water, since I have yet to reconnect the pump. We paint everything stark white, and by July if the gods are benevolent the evil-smelling shanty will dry out and be habitable again. The day turns into a hot Sunday afternoon, and I gaze at the sleeping naked form of my wife stretched out languorously on the porch. I wonder if she's pregnant. A chickadee is looping

Hanging out at Alley's on Memorial Day, and another summer begins

65

Catch it

Watch it

out the same monotonous code and overhead a huge red-tail hawk is circling, circling, looking for her lunch. Memorial Day weekend: The Island is just turning to green, the roads and beaches are empty of tourists and cars, and life is quiet, peaceful, beautifully still.

June 2 My friend Neegus shows up, an artist who lives with his wife at the far end of a bad road in Gay Head. Once again he wintered up-Island and now has emerged, as usual, somewhat dazed. All those months with no social life, nothing to do but brood. Brooding is one of those things the up-Island demimonde does best. In the winter Neegus says he's lucky if he sees anybody besides his wife and the RFD postmistress during the course of a week. Neegus is feeling somewhat exalted today, since he (like most of the up-Island organic gardeners) just finished putting in his marijuana crop. All spring Vineyard Bohemia has been reading the cannabis literature, swapping arcane notes and techniques, arguing about how early to plant and how tight to trim the shake and how to tenderly doctor a *sensimilla* flower. These things can take on a terrible importance when one has been brooding for nine months. Neegus takes us to his family's private beach, a broad white silicate strand not far from Zack's Cliffs, whose stately beauty is one of the few things that can stun my wife into absolute silence. We gambol and

Ride that tide and go with the flow.

Summer reading

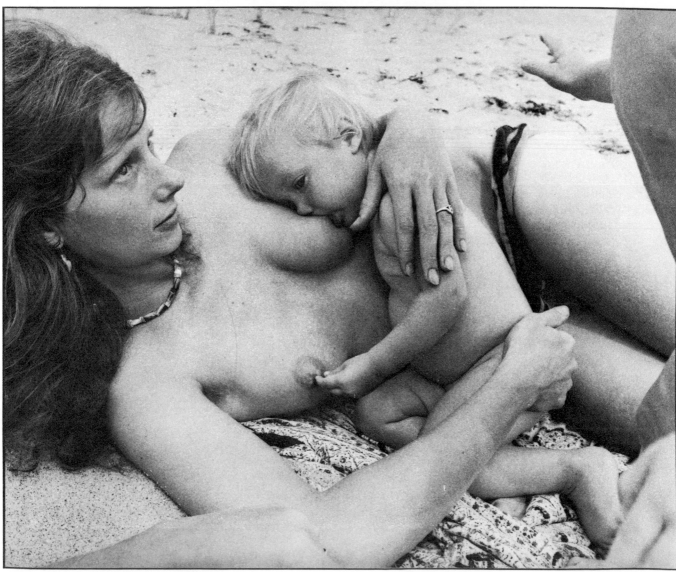

Quansoo ladies

An intense contest

plunge nude through the high chilly breakers and let the pre-equinox sun bake us silly until a wild-card series of bloated fog banks rolls in from the Atlantic and sends us back to Neegus's wood stove, clutching our towels around us.

June 10 On Saturday nights, the Vineyard demimonde gets together to eat and play music. Tonight we're invited to a teepee along Tiah's Cove. Our host is up-Island Pierre, former New York fashion model turned white dreadlocks and avant-garde record producer, and royal consort Heloise, a Franco-Hungarian chanteuse and raving beauty. They are the Soho/Boho aesthetic personified on the Vineyard. Always a pleasure to see them. Dinner is three kinds of raw fish and rice rolled in comfrey leaves, cheese from their cow Leopoldine, fried breaded tofu, liqueurs, cakes, and tea — everything piquant, delicate, perfectly cooked. Vineyard demimondaines know how to live. Big spliffs rolled out of five-pound bags of Quenames Red, Quansoo Blue, Gay Head Green, and blond Lebanese hashish. Reggae tapes (the latest singles) and the usual esoteric visuals and campfire hallucinations. There're a dozen of us around the fire, spread on buffalo robes; everyone's

been everywhere and everyone brought back drums — sensual draboogas from Morocco, *akete* drums from Jamaica, roped talking drums from Sierra Leone, rapping Indian tablas. The women ease out the rattles and flutes and suddenly it's midnight, the fog outside is thick and looming, but it's bone dry in the teepee and . . . *we're jamming*. Bup chu wadda-da.

June 15 My general take on the Vineyard is as follows: down-Island is suburbanized and overpoliced. Up-Island is in its last days as real country towns, even in winter. Chilmark and Gay Head are being slowly but inexorably built up, and although very little of the Island, as one can see from the air, is actually developed, each new house or driveway seems an intrusion, a small annoying pain. It must be sad for the older natives. On the other hand, maybe it's a relief from their classic isolation and the truly major-league alcoholism that breeds there in the wintertime.

June 21 Solstice. First day of summer. A blinding star blasts out of blue-turns-to-gray clouds and awakens me at 5 A.M. Later that day spent under blistering white-hot June sun at good old Jungle Beach, a demimonde paradise.

Ozzie Fischer, his men and machine

This morning the beach was cut in half by a huge tidal cut that drained Chilmark Pond when the tide went out again. Trying to cross this flowing river I sank up to my neck, soaking my trousers and the spliff in my pocket. My wife saved our lunch by bundling it up and balancing it on her head as she gracefully waded through an ankle-deep ford to the other bank. We thereupon roast our flesh in coconut grease and oil of aloe until Sol sends us reeling to the languor of a beach tent made of our red checkered tablecloth and driftwood. It's Sunday morning; the voluptuous shapes of nude demimondaines mingle with each other, angling for a bit of that cool orange juice, a bit of that passing pipe, or the Arts and Leisure section of the Sunday *Times*. The ocean is warmer than usual this early in the summer, and the body surfers are out in force, making the most of the perfect thirty-inch curls that hurl you back at the beach like a rocket if you catch it right and ride the wind in your chest like a sleigh down a snowy hill. Eat, lounge, gossip, watch the curves and breasts and handsome tan muscles of the demimonde and corporate captains alike. Who was that fool who said that nude beaches weren't sexy? The children splash and dive in the foam like brown seals and screech like the gulls. The children bathe till they're blue and weep when their mothers separate them from the chattering spell of the sea.

June 25 An impeccable weekend, the first of summer. A pleasure to be aimlessly wandering the beaches again. The windless glare of these late solstice days, the radiational cooling in the twilight evening, and the cloudless orange-and-purple sunsets. The night air is frosty in expectation of a cool and almost unbearably starry evening. Look up at the winking curtain of light that the ocean night lets you sight, and you feel like nothing, like nothing at all.

July 1 I'm wallowing like a walrus in the shallow foam over at Jungle Beach as two young nudes walk by. The blond Reubens nudges the thin dark Modigliani strolling next to her and points to a red starfish they almost stepped on.

"Ugh," groaned the Modigliani. "Does it bite?"

"No," answered the bounteous Reubens, "but it *smells.*"

July 5 Every now and then we struggle over an abandoned cowpath and through a thorny briar patch to get to a hidden white-sand beach on Menemsha Pond. The pond is even warmer than the warming sea, and we watch the particolored triangles of the Sunfish and Laser fleets competing against each other; we swim among blissful peace, and the gentle blue hills around the pond keep away the wind. They also

provided shelter for the Vineyard's aboriginal demimonde; the little rills around these ponds are the sites of some of the oldest human habitation yet found on the East Coast. Today my dogs were digging furiously at a section of crumbling black bank, and when I waded over to see what they were about, I picked up a shining, lustrous quartz arrowhead, small and exquisitely formed. What a prize! I shouted like a demento, scaring the dogs, holding my artifact up to the sun and praying a thankful greeting to the generous ancestral spirits of this holy place.

July 8 The Keith Farm is an imaginary landscape somewhere in Chilmark. Pasture and ponds are amiably shared by Ozzie Fischer's cattle and dawdling flocks of migrating Canada geese. When I sit on his stone wall watching Ozzie cutting hay (a week late due to the rains) and the sun's reflection off the pond burns into my eyes, it all seems too good to be true.

Gay Head Green

Caught in the act of Guerrilla-Tennis

July 20 Guerrilla-tennis is a game you have to play up-Island before you play guerrilla-tennis. This is because in Gay Head and Chilmark there are less than two dozen courts for a population of about ten thousand, and all but seven of them are absolutely private. Vineyard Bohemians aren't as a rule members of the Chilmark Community Center, so that rules out six courts right away. Therefore the only way to play is to abuse your friendships with up-Island swells who have their own surfaces and are liberal enough to allow you to play. But the greatest, most masterful guerrilla-tennis partisans actually go and sneak on the courts of people they don't even know, tennis courts so isolated in the scrub oak and Highmark brush that it's usually safe to play early in the morning and at cocktail time. It helps to be able to balance half a dozen four-figure padlock combinations in your head, so that, say, if you want to sneak on Saxman's court on Lobsterville Road, you're not beating your brains worrying her lock with the combo to the gorgeous turn-of-the-century court up above Windy Gates in Chilmark. To be a guerrilla-tennis bum, one needs a high put-down threshold. Nothing is more painful to a prosperous

Wall Street lawyer who summers on the Vineyard than to be escorting his similarly white-clad tennis guests down a shady lane to his own exquisitely expensive court only to behold the sight of a quartet of motley seminude up-Island hobos hacking away blissfully on his turf. Great bellows of outrage, but never any violence. Once Neegus and I and our wives were playing *tennis noir* up at the Dump Courts when some properly attired stockbrokers and their old ladies showed up to play. I was playing naked in my sneaks and Mrs. Neegus was bare-breasted. They looked upon us with psychotic horror and we yukked it up, laughed it off, and got our things ready to go. One of the matrons had the temerity to ask who we were. "Well," Neegus lied, "our friends the Whites said we could use their court this afternoon." Matron glanced furtively at our perspiring, exposed flesh. "Oh dear," she whimped, "I'm so afraid that we're just not *doing* that this year." At least she was polite.

July 25 The Vineyard is perfect for feuds. On an island everyone knows almost everything about everybody. Rumor and gossip are the lingua franca. Maybe it's the fresh air, but Vineyarders are extremely cranky. Since there's little to occupy oneself with other than creative brooding, a good feud can be the basis of an epic interpersonal relationship involving not only the feudees but all of one's friends as well. Neighbors have been known to burn each other out over minor boundary disputes. A Conan Doylesque gang of arsonist-dwarves was broken up in Chilmark a few years ago.

Ocean sunsets make up for the occasional weird vibe from your neighbor. Don't be a paranoid, just look up. At nine minutes to nine there's a small patch of pure crimson on the horizon line. Nothing much, and you turn your head away to look for the dogs. When you turn back no more than ten seconds has elapsed, but the whole sky is afire in a stupefying display of vermilion evening pyrotechnicolor. In the foreground lie the five purple Elizabeths, low and comfortably nestled into a coral red sea. Naushon, the largest, is a mini-Vineyard in landscape and temperament, and the private preserve of one of the old China trade families. It looks so placid and pristine at this hour of the day, and all one can do is look on in yearning.

July 28 Not much happening at night up-Island. These are this evening's choices: hanging out at Squid Row, Menemsha, checking out the action on the stink pots; the questionable pleasures of the Hot Tin Roof; eight bad movies down-Island or the bucolic pleasures of the toast of Oak Bluffs, the Ritz Cafe, fuzzy reception of Rhode Island television, arguably the worst in the world. Fortunately Neegus calls up with threats of a barbecue down at Squibnocket,

*Getting
clayed*

and he shows up with huge steaks of fresh salmon and swordfish and a case of cold beer (rare, since up-Island is still dry), and we eat like fools, get grit in our teeth, toast the bulbous red waxing moon.

July 29 This night there was a complete and ominous and utter silence in the still air for three hours before all hell broke loose. The storm came in across South Beach in awesome rolling thunderballs, a *tsunami* of violent noise amid ragged shards of white-hot light. The rain was so heavy and tough that it blew out the power in Chilmark and Gay Head, and we cowered at the thought of floating down our colline in the ruins of our shack. Later, when a northwestern breeze blew the mess back out to sea and the stars came out, it seemed silly to be frightened; a dramatic landscape brews dramatic, or at least overdramatized, ideas.

August 1 Mysteriously, on this date every year, the roads up-Island fill with New York license plates, as if much of the Upper East Side and the better part of Westchester has come up for the month. At the little Chilmark grocery, prices are rather high this year. One store has a plan where two or three families can get together and buy shares in a tomato or a zucchini. The SEC is reportedly investigating.

August 10 Six days of foul weather and everyone is getting in plenty of brooding. The days start out foggy, annoying, wispy little smoke, and you think it's going to burn off. You sort of get ready for the beach. But the only place it burns off is Lambert's Cove — up-Island it's

another warm, damp pea-souper all day. After a week of this, nerves are frayed and drugs become scarce. Monotony is broken by Djanet selling a painting and Terry getting four swordfish and Eddie Guitar getting home off a three-month tour with the Isley Brothers, all in the same day, and everybody shows up at the Home Port for the celebration. Then back to Studio Do in Gay Head for tapes of rockers and dancing, and as the sun comes up for the first time in a week the surviving remnant of last night's demimonde hoots and hollers in relief and grateful derision.

August 15 A blessed Bermuda high is pumping luscious tropical air into our system; today a blue-knife-horizon beach day. We cross the sand and walk out through the warm, ecstatic shallows toward the low tide in the distance. Five minutes later we're only up to our knees. Back on the beach our party is almost invisible, dwarfed by the stately blond bluffs streaked with gray veins of clay and falls and faults dotted with green vegetation. We rinse the drying salt with the fresh water we've brought and pass the hot afternoon wallowing in the gray goo of the warm clay pits. It's called *getting clayed,* and after you rinse the baked mud off your skin with a plunge into the waves, you feel like a godling or a wild spirit. In the daytime it's too hot for houses; tents and teepees sprout up and people forget about four walls while the weather holds. The breeziness of tent life, open to the brisk air of the Atlantic winds, must be one of the greatest pleasures of our lives.

A portrait at the fair

Been too long at the fair

August 17 Stayed too long at the fair. The Dukes County Agricultural Fair, that is. Persistent postexit symptoms include gruesome indigestion and a relentless ringing in the ears. Consumed were tempura, clams, corn, chowder, shrimps, fried crispy-dough, gallons of lemonade. *Gallons.* I always gravitate to the hard-core carny scene — pitch-penny and magnet games, fifty cents to throw darts at Farrah Fawcett's anatomy on a poster, the Ferris wheel, the merry-go-round, the tilt-a-puke. Widespread depression and glowing blue light of Rhode Island TV in the Gypsy trailer encampment parked hard by the fairway. I remember in Ibiza, the *guardia* wouldn't let the Spanish Gypsies off the ferry for the festival of the local saint. Here everybody revels in the sweet smell of country dusk and frying oil.

The famous horsepull contest

Fair competition

August 21 Gay Head is the only place where the Indians won. The tribe still has the cliffs and the herring run and is making enough trouble so it's hard to get a mortgage in the place. The Wampanoag Tribal Council has sued for the town lands, and a lot of people hope they get away with it. Some of my younger Wampanoag friends still secretly maintain the cult of the giant Moshup, the old coastal god who could wrest whales from Vineyard Sound and who took a powder when the first Christian missionaries showed up in the seventeenth century. They say Moshup gripped his wife, Olesquant, under his arm and took off at a dead run from the Gay Head cliffs, disappeared over the horizon, and met an ambiguous fate. Moshup was powerful in the old days and his name pops up (sometimes as Moosup) as place names and names of streams and roads all over Connecticut and eastern New York. My friend Buddy lives over near Moshup Trail. He's chairman of the Gay Head selectmen, a scalloper and swordfisherman, a traveler and man of the world. He and his brothers run around Gay Head in a fleet of BMWs and quietly direct the natural order of things. Things are looking good for Gay Head, but the days of the up-Island demimonde may be definitely numbered. Mrs. Onassis is moving in, and up-Island finally could get really chic after all these years of eccentric obscurity. Buddy says he's going to do some scalloping for a while and, things being what they are in Gay Head these days, he figures to winter in Jamaica on his old lady's two-acre farm and do some serious cooling out. Gay Headers, especially the Indians, love to leave Gay Head. But they always seem to equally love coming back.

September 6 Labor Day brings on the usual chilly nights and culture shock. Within the space of seventy-two hours, the Island's population plummets by thirty thousand souls, due to massive migration to the mainland. All of a sudden you can get a table in the restaurants, drive right up to the beach, and guerrilla-tennis strategies become obsolete. One trespasses on the most exclusive courts with arrogant impunity. The ocean, baking all summer, provides all the pleasures of a warm saline bath, and at night Venus shows herself like a street lamp in the western sky.

September 20 Best time of the year. Up-Island is hinting at turning a deep russet, a flaming sienna almost surreal against the impossible blue of the sea. The season is over and the Islanders are getting back to autumnal brooding again. Down in West Tisbury they have a horse race and someone always sets up a pari-mutuel betting window off to the side of the

Buddy Vanderhoop and family

pasture; everyone gets drunk and has a good time. This afternoon the up-Island agronomists were trying to judge the winner of the annual Anarchy Cup for best cannabis crop. The judges puffed until they were cross-eyed and their brains had turned to spinach, and then awarded the trophy to the mistress of Tea Lane Farm for her magical herb, Chilmark Headache.

October 1

Time to close it down for another winter. Pull the pump, lay out the mouse poison (the rodents find this a huge joke), turn off the phone, gas, and power, and hope the winter doesn't blow this shed into Quitsa Pond. Up-Island that portion of the demimonde that has decided to try to stick it out for another winter moves into the heated summer houses at reduced rent or reinforces their summer shacks with Fiberglas, wood stoves, and extra blankets. When the Island is bare of leaves and covered with snow, only then can one really get the lay of the land, its hidden paths and geosynclines. It's an aspect of this place summer people can never get to know.

Of course, not all the undergroundites stay the winter. Some hop to other isles in more tropical climes — Hawaii, Formentera, Jamaica, Key West. Some go back to the real world and toil at real jobs in order to sustain their Vineyard *jones*, that maddening addiction that works itself up every spring, when the goddess Aquinnah smiles benevolently, maternally, upon the slowly greening island and it's time to get another year's crop in.

Stephen Davis, thirty-one, is an up-Island summer resident who writes frequently about music, Morocco, Jamaica, and the Vineyard. His pieces have appeared in Rolling Stone, The New York Times Magazine, New Age, Green Mountain Post, High Times, Oui, *and* Geo. *He is the author of* Reggae Bloodlines *(1977) and is currently writing a novel about up-Island summers. Aside from writing, Stephen spends much of his time playing with his young daughter Lily Aisha, playing guerrilla-tennis, and brooding.*

A late fall excursion to Jungle Beach

THE LEGEND OF OAK BLUFFS

Dorothy West

It was once called Squash Meadow, this down-Island town, a fine dimension of accommodating land, rich for farming, with fields of native squash for Indian hands to harvest when fall nudged the nodding earth toward its winter sleep.

It was the English who named the fertile tract Squash Meadow, and the pond that nourished it Squash Meadow Pond, "squash" distilled from the longer Algonquin word for it. Those names are now buried in archives, the freshwater pond long opened to the sea and called Lake Anthony, Squash Meadow turned into a town of steamboat landings, gingerbread cottages, and summer children on flying horses, whirling round and round in the realm of forever remembering.

The Englishman who fathered the birth of Squash Meadow was Thomas Mayhew of Watertown, a merchant by trade, knowing a bargain when he saw one. He bought Martha's Vineyard, Nantucket, and the Elizabeth Islands from two Englishmen with royal grants for fifty pounds. To Mayhew the land that would sustain a man best seemed to be Martha's Vineyard, the name itself — for it was always so named — a guarantee of enduring benignity. His son, Thomas, Jr., and a group of his friends bought their farm and forest tools and hunting guns, and shaped a settlement out of the eastern end of the island, calling it Great Harbour, and, in time, Edgartown.

In 1642 John Daggett, also English-born and a Watertown neighbor of Mayhew who was now taking part in the island adventure, purchased from Mayhew the five hundred acres of farmland known as Squash Meadow. Sometime thereafter his son, Joseph, having turned twenty and taken an Indian bride, felt ready to add another notch to his manhood with the stewardship of the Squash Meadow property.

Joseph became the first white man to build in Oak Bluffs, his squat, square house hard wrestled from oak and pine. He stayed on Squash Farm until the land was proud, his house was tight, his children flourishing. There was a new settlement called Takemmy, later to be the township of Tisbury. Joseph itched to move on to new ground, to feel its soil, to test its streams. His father had died and Squash Meadow was his inheritance. The choice was his to keep or sell. He sold it in several parcels. Among the new owners was one Simeon Butler, whose parcel included the beautiful grove that one day would be called the Camp Ground, a place whose future would be determined by religion.

The colony's established church was the Congregational Church in Great Harbour until 1795, when an evangelist named Jesse Lee, the father of New England Methodism, came to spread the new faith to a small gathering that numbered more curious than converts. But the scraggly meetings continued, sometimes in a borrowed hall, sometimes in a borrowed house. Eventually week-long meetings were held on the grove during summer months and the numbers continued to grow. There were families who came two weeks before the meetings got under way and stayed two weeks after the closing, writing the association in

The way it was down Circuit Avenue at the turn of the century

advance of their coming to secure a favorite location beside familiar neighbors who were making the same request. Their children looked forward to playing together, to wading in the lake, to climbing trees, to eating together camp-style outdoors. Grown-ups and children alike began to look forward to escaping the city heat for a month or so on a breeze-swept island, mixing prayer and innocent pleasure. These were the first summer people, though they would have been startled by that appellation. They had never taken vacations, as had few Americans, and they did not yet know they were doing it now.

With the association's permission the regulars began to build small board structures, not yet resembling the gingerbread cottages, but at least they could tell one board structure from another by some individual touch.

The gingerbread cottages began to be built around 1860, the cottages being owned by the families who built them, but the land, then and now, leased from the association for one hundred years. The association had received its charter from the Massachusetts legislature that year.

In that same period of time a huge amphitheater

of sail cloth containing three thousand yards of canvas was erected in the center of the grove. In 1870 it was replaced by the huge iron tabernacle that was a wonder in its day.

The Baptists were the second-largest denomination on the Vineyard. They had come as missionaries to convert the Indians, then added the white population as souls in need of proselytizing. The Baptists did not meet the same resistance from the missionary Mayhews as had the Methodists, which may have been an indication that their raids on the Congregationalists did not yield the same harvest.

The success of the Methodist camp meeting emboldened the Baptists to approach the Methodists to suggest a summer coalition, the grove to be shared, the ministers alternated. The Methodists preferred to keep a good thing to themselves.

The Vineyard Grove Company was one of many real-estate ventures. Boardinghouses and eating places began to border the Camp Ground to serve the onslaught of visitors coming not so much to seek a spiritual place in God's grace but to seek a summer place in his garden.

The Oak Bluffs bandstand silhouetted at Ocean Park

and a bizarre tree nearby.

A group of wealthy mainland men purchased the land between the Camp Ground and the sea, and incorporated themselves into the Oak Bluffs Land and Wharf Company. They called that area Oak Bluffs, and laid out streets and avenues and lovely parks. Somewhere along this point the Camp Ground Association enclosed its thirty-six acres behind a seven-foot-high picket fence to separate the sacred from the noisy hordes of the secular.

There were now three prosperous summer settlements: the Camp Ground; the Highlands, its Baptist Temple the centerpiece of a circle of cottages, continuously extending; and Oak Bluffs,

with its waterfront of magnificent cottages, its elaborate hotels, its main street shops.

The tax money flowing into Edgartown was considerable, with the county seat complacently accepting it and doing nothing to deserve it. Oak Bluffs' nearest neighbor, Tisbury, was not more than a mile away, but the only access was by boat, a slow and inconvenient arrangement. Edgartown refused to build a bridge between the towns. But after much debate, petitioners presented a bill to the Massachusetts General Court compelling the county commissioners to build the bridge. Edgartown fought the petition, lost, and the bridge

*A telephoto view of various porches
along New York Avenue.*

was built.

In the 1880s the first Portuguese settlement burgeoned in Oak Bluffs on rich land planted for market gardening. The area in which they lived was bound by Dukes County Avenue and County Road, and Vineyard Avenue and School Street.

The summer cottagers bought everything the Portuguese planting brought forth, as did the hotel, the boardinghouses, the restaurants. A prized crop was flowers. There was a feast of flowers. The summer people packed their porches and parlors. It seemed to be a summer pastime to see how many flower baskets and vases could squeeze into a given space.

There were spring and summer jobs for every able Portuguese, road work, opening cottages, readying lawns and yards, meeting the many boats, and carrying baggage to nearby houses or hotels. Women did housework, and there were those who did fine hand laundry. The summer ladies would ride through the Portuguese enclave looking for a sign that said "Fine Hand Laundry." Those were the years when starched clothes were a mark of distinction.

The summer people were Republican and reluctant to hire anyone who was not. They had no hesitation in asking a job-seeker about his politics. The Portuguese understood the question's intent. They did not want the summer jobs slammed shut in their faces, and winter's hunger to howl at their door. They said they were Republican, and in the next voter registration made sure that they were so inscribed. The town and the Island are still Republican.

Manuel De Bettencourt — that surname still prevalent in its many branches — had been one of the first to own land in the Portuguese settlement. In many ways he was the liaison between the English and the Portuguese cultures, neither at odds with the other, both loosely joined in a pragmatic union of mutual need.

Manuel and Anna, his wife, had managed everything except a gift in the name of God. It troubled them. They and the others from the Azores who had settled on this bountiful land had much to be thankful for, and no sacred place in which to give thanks together. In their very own house, in their rarely used parlor, they made room for that sacred place. Manuel wrote to his former parish in New Bedford, asking with proper humility if there was some mainland priest who would come to say Mass whatever Sunday he could spare the time.

And so it was that every two weeks a priest arrived from the mainland. Then there began to be a feeling of loss, of double loss on the alternate Sundays. Like a rising chorus, talk of building a church began in a muted way, then soared to a crescendo. Quickly the talk turned into tithes. A building fund was started, swelled. A Catholic manservant purchased a building lot just around the corner from Manuel's house and donated the lot to the cause.

In a miracle of time the church was built and called the Sacred Heart. Across the street there was soon to be the Sacred Heart Rectory and the joyous affirmation of a priest in residence. The old church is now the Sacred Heart Parish Hall. A larger, more centrally located church is Our Lady Star of the Sea, its congregation, year-round and summer, of every social stratum, with an easy mingling of races.

The twenties were in giant-size bloom on the Island. Summer money fell like rain on all the towns, especially the down-Island towns, and notably Oak Bluffs, with its accessibility to steamboat landings, with its carriages and automobiles for hire, its Tivoli dance hall, its moving-picture houses, its bandstand in the park, and the Methodist Tabernacle no longer a hotbed of fiery evangelists, but still an impressive place of assembly, with important guest speakers on a latitude of topics, and musical performances with gifted artists, and the magical, lantern-lit Illumination Night, as unique an experience as can be had.

Then it was 1929, and the stock market crash, and on its heels, the Depression. And for the decade following the crash Oak Bluffs suffered a lingering sickness of meager summers. It was the town hardest hit because it was the town whose summer business had been its only business. The great houses stood empty, too large to run without servants, and too few, if any, families who could still afford a staff. The hotels and shops that struggled to stay open were barely staying alive. "For Sale" signs were everywhere, and there were no buyers. Those half-empty steamers discharged from their decks only those summer arrivals whose cottages had been family-owned into the fourth generation. They could not deny these fourth-generation children their birthright to an island summer and break the chain of privilege.

The non-WASPs were of such slight numerical strength that they had never come close to rocking the boat. Nor had they tried. They had kept a low profile, especially the little pockets of vacationing black Bostonians. It was a fine accomplishment for these early comers to the island to own summer cottages, whatever their size, whatever their lack of inside conveniences. Kerosene lamps cast a lovely soft light. The backyard pump poured water sweeter than any from an indoor faucet.

That they could afford a cottage at all, that a black man could send his wife and children on a summer vacation was a clear indication that he had made a profitable place for himself in the white world, vaulting whatever color bar stood in his way.

The tabernacle

His motivations were a fierce sense of family and a proud acknowledgment of his role as its head.

In the Depression years there were enough of them established as summer residents to constitute a definable colony, devoutly committed to a yearly return at whatever sacrifice of winter's priorities, with whatever pared amount of vacation money, and with the most careful piecing together of summer clothes.

They were among that legion that adds adherents every summer, those who find the Island irresistible, and have to set foot on its waiting shore, and sift the white sand in a cupped hand, and smell the salt tang of the sea. This is the rite that purges them of all evil.

The genesis of the black colony was no more than a dozen families. From that group of cottagers the colony made slow but pervasive growth, drawing its component parts of acceptable people from Boston, New York, Philadelphia, Washington, and a scattering of other certifiable cities, excluding the Deep South cities because of an obsessive fear that the Deep South people might bring their attitudes of uncertainty to a place where blacks did not hang back to let the whites go first.

With Pearl Harbor, prosperity zoomed from high-rise to hovel, money became a common commodity, and those who had never had a cent to spare could look beyond the landlord's outstretched hand. New economic classes emerged and rapidly became aware that there were people in established classes who lived lives of more variety than city streets and subway benches. The new partakers of prosperity did not know what a day in the country looked like but now had the means to find out.

Oak Bluffs received its share of seekers of the good life. And the good life had many definitions. It was a time of experimentation, of trial and error, an occasional triumph, adjustment or disengagement, observed behavior abided by or rejected.

There were blacks who tried the Island once, and came no more. They were done in by the fog, and the creepy feeling, and the foghorn making mournful sounds all night. And the beaches, the whole place surrounded by beaches. When you've seen one, the others don't look any different. And the woods. When you've seen one tree, you've seen the rest of the forest. A dirt road goes nowhere. What do you do for excitement? Dullsville.

But the others found more than they ever hoped that they would find. A place where they could stand to full size. The town was right for them, and the time of their coming was right for the town. The wave of whites washed across the whole island, but the blacks settled where the way had been charted.

They made a massive imprint. They bought the big neglected houses, and other long-empty cottages, lifted their sagging facades, put in new

*A leap into the choppy waters
at Oak Bluffs Beach*

Gingerbread cottages get their annual Spring cleaning.

plumbing and wiring, scrubbed and polished and painted. The more improvements they made, the more they paid in taxes and increased the town's returns.

In the early eighties the old guard, the originals, are only remainders, a vanishing though unvanquished group, once labeled the Forty; forty women serenely secure who, with their husbands, were on everybody's party lists, those big August parties when the husbands who could afford a longer stay than a weekend took a two-week vacation which, as time passed and incomes doubled, would extend to the standard month.

In the main they were always a professional group, a pattern of people whose occupations in the fields of white predominance demanded a confident self-image, which enlarged their worldliness and gave strong support to their

Chortling on the porch.

observation that summer vacations were the color of green money. Black money, Jewish money, Irish money here were just as green as high-and-mighty money, though maybe not as old and honorable or as carefully used.

In the upper strata of black families, loyalty, and, almost concomitantly, group loyalty are chiseled into their earliest consciousness. If these loyalties were once regional, it was because the automobile had not yet become a national necessity, nor was plane travel a common practice. Now from anywhere to everywhere is only a matter of hours. On the Island, in particular Oak Bluffs, the bonding of blacks comes into sharpest focus.

There are some who think that these blacks sprang full grown from the earth into preordained postures of success. No, their advantage was that their forebears came out of slavery with a fierce will to make up for lost time, and few descendants have let that momentum slacken.

Oak Bluffs is an archetype of the art of people living together where their similarities are points of contact and their differences are intriguing regions to explore. Almost everyone, summer or year-round resident, has friends of every race and every level of experience. The few and fragile summer strongholds of resistance still remaining are now anachronisms. If the best is yet to come, the present will blend with it beautifully.

Dressed for the occasion

Illumination Eve

Oak Bluffs as it is today;
jumbled, funky and basically happy

Dorothy West is a prominent member of the black community in Oak Bluffs. She writes a weekly column about that town for the Vineyard Gazette *and has written a novel,* Living Is Easy. *She has also written several stories using the Vineyard as a backdrop. Dorothy is a charismatic woman who gains much joy out of life's simple pleasures.*

VINEYARD PASSAGE
Robert Brustein

I spent my first summer on Martha's Vineyard three months after I was married. During our second summer on the island, my wife was pregnant. And by our third summer, following the birth of our son, Daniel, we had taken up residence in the house we had bought in Lambert's Cove. Place and family are inextricable on this island, and we measure our years by the passage of our summers.

I have lived in many cities, both in the United States and abroad. I was born and raised in New York. I have endured the past thirteen years in New Haven. But while it would be indulgent to speak of home when speaking of an island where we have spent only one sixth of each year for the past fifteen years, nevertheless Martha's Vineyard has been the

and architecture that have accompanied our years on the Vineyard. The original A frame of our early-nineteenth-century house has now been joined by L's and H's, as we added new bedrooms, porches, and a dining room to accommodate our growing family. The willow we planted some distance away when we first purchased our house now droops over the roof of our new kitchen wing, raising fears that it might soon seek nourishment in the water pipes of our sink. The blue spruce we planted at the same time, which now blocks our entrance to the shed, is mature enough to convince us that our suspicions were correct, and it is green. The sassafras grove has multiplied like the weed it is, and the myrtle cover spreads over the land like a counterpane. In my walks, I frequently come upon some token of things past — a piece of a toy lawnmower with which my baby son used to imitate his father's labors, the rubber tire of a wheelbarrow, a remnant of the stone wall we moved some fifty

The Brustein expanse

one geographical constant in the hearts of a family that values emotional constancy. My son's annual leaps in height are recorded in pencil against the doorjamb of our bedroom. A crude cross in black ink on our living-room wall signifies a ferocious fight between my wife and me, six years ago, over the casting of a play. Down the hill from the house in the woods, there still stands the remains of a platform built by my stepson as the floor of a tent in which he lived for one summer.

The examples suggest, however, that in the midst of this pastoral stability lies the inevitable pattern of change, and in my seasonal role of summer squire, traversing my land as an excuse to avoid my work, I often contemplate the alterations in nature

feet north when we acquired another acre.

How curious our Vineyard life has been, then, as if we had spent here one long summer of fifteen years' duration, during which our children had grown, our bodies and faces had aged, our architecture had expanded, our vegetation had increased. A long summer of time in which, year after year, we had renewed with friends strong relationships that were suspended during the winter, found new fishing holes, decided not to risk lobster pots again, worked on the boat and failed to get the fanbelt tightened, lost the oil in the compass and failed to replace it, watched the sea grass accumulate on the hull and failed to scrape it off, lived with a radio that received but couldn't

Unloading sea scallops in Edgartown

transmit, drank a little more, ate a little less, and finally reached the point where we could compare the summer's weather with a period of a decade past and agree with those who found it to be deteriorating.

What else had changed? The placement of the clams in Tashmoo Pond — but not my pleasure in digging for them. Indeed, I have never fully understood why clamming in Tashmoo has constituted the single most delicious activity of my Vineyard summer, more even than the round-robin tennis matches on the private courts of friends, or that first brisk exhilarating dip into the July waters of South Beach, or that outdoor shower on a sun-kissing day. Let me tell you about the clamming. I start out from the mooring in Vineyard Harbor on my twenty-one-foot Wasque, shared in ownership with the Styrons. I am past the Chop in ten minutes,

at the mouth of Tashmoo Channel in twenty. The engine is cut almost to idling as the current pushes against the slight forward movement in the channel. I throw an anchor on Milton Gordon's beach, and, with a yellow plastic bucket in hand, go to my secret place for clams. As I squat in the water at low tide, I can just see Milton's osprey feeding its young, the gulls wheeling over Tashmoo Beach, a solitary black duck in flight. I scratch through the sand and muck. A crab pinches my finger and I draw away in pain. I am scrabbling the sand now with my ten fingers and my ten toes. A hard object responds to my touch — a nice-sized cherrystone. There is a tiny clam nearby it — I heave it farther into the pond. I cut my finger on an open shell (a common hazard of clamming) and suck the blood. In an hour, I have collected enough for spaghetti pesto, to be made from Lillian's excellent recipe, or

*Easy clamming in the shallows
of Sengekontacket.*

A tidal mooring

Late spring afternoon

for stuffed clams, or for an appetizer of clams on the half shell for a party of eight. I have enough in my bucket, but a frenzy of greed has overtaken me. I can't stop clamming. Deciding to take only four more, I break my promise when I come upon five in one small area. I understand gambling now, and acquisition, and remember how hard it was to give up cigarettes. I am in the grip of a habit, and I love it. The return trip to Vineyard Haven, the current behind me, planing on the waves, is the memory that I retain most vividly in the long winter to come.

The Vineyard, then, is my world of growth and of stability, the capacity for change and the capacity for permanence. It represents the single season when work and pleasure, society and privacy conjoin in perfect harmony. T. S. Eliot's lady measured out her life in coffee spoons. I, much luckier, have measured out my own in Vineyard summers. The sound of the West Chop foghorn, the cries of children in Seth's Pond, the barking of a faraway dog, the topping of trees in Mohu, my neighbor naked on his tractor tilling the soil of his meadow, the goofy pigeon-toed quail scurrying in a panic as we come up our dusty driveway, the

mouse droppings that inevitably appear upon the stove if we leave the house for more than three days, the phallic mushrooms that bloom near my study after a night of hard rain — these and much, much more are the images of my passage, the tokens of my sojourn on this island of summer and of change.

Robert Brustein spends his Vineyard summers on Lambert's Cove, and along with Styron, Hart, Buchwald, and Lang (among others) is a member of the author's tennis contingent. He can often be found on his way to the clamming grounds as well. Mr. Brustein was, for many years, the dean of the Yale Drama School, and now is the director of the Loeb Theater of Harvard. As well as his life in the theater, he is an accomplished author and noted drama critic, with such titles as Seasons of Discontent, The Theater of Revolt, Revolution as Theater, *and* The Culture Watch.

A fisherman's tableau in Chilmark

Lobster crates on the standby line in Menemsha

*Menemsha sunsets are a must, except when
a good cocktail party is in progress.*

WHISKEY SOUR
Daniel Lang

I don't like cocktail parties anywhere, and on the Vineyard I like them even less. The fault's my own. I have illusions about the Vineyard. I think of it as an oasis for recollecting in tranquillity, as a spot for getting away from urban artificialities. I've spent twenty-five summers on the Vineyard, so I should know better, but the Island's beauty sustains the illusions and they just won't go away. On the Vineyard, cocktail parties strike me as faintly sacrilegious, especially since they take place in the late afternoon. That's when I know my favorite summer hours. It's then that, up-Island, where I have a place, I can watch the sun begin its slow descent into the waters of Menemsha Bight, shedding fire on the Elizabeth Islands, fire that pales the wheeling beams of the Gay Head lighthouse; well after the sun has dipped below the horizon, the sky is left aglow — by whom, by what? — with a lingering aftermath of unknown colors arranged in unknown patterns. It's in the late afternoon, too, that one may wander the narrow pier at Menemsha, silently welcoming the homecoming commercial vessels, their hearty, high-booted crews unloading swordfish while gulls, shrieking wildly, circle low for a chance at sampling the huge carcasses. And it's toward twilight, far from the sound of rattling ice cubes, that one is able to take stock quietly of what the Island day has already brought — beach, tennis, work — and to contemplate what the oncoming night may hold in store — the whippoorwill's rhythmic call, the lullaby of a distant buoy's bell, perhaps a predawn rainstorm that will end with a fresh wafting of the Island's fragrant air.

But to get back to those cocktail parties. Every day, as at other resorts, a rash of them breaks out, up-Island and down, from Gay Head to Edgartown, in houses large and small. For the most part, the gatherings are crowded affairs, excursions in claustrophobia; often an overflow of guests spills out onto the host's lawn. (Several years ago, *The New Yorker* ran a full-page cartoon showing a cocktail party in progress on an immense lawn that was jammed with guests, one of whom was telling the host, "Congratulations, Larry! It's unquestionably the biggest party ever held on Martha's Vineyard.") When I first came to the Vineyard, I fell in with the cocktail-party mode on the theory that I was doing as the Romans did. It wasn't long, though, before I forgot all about Rome, and now it's seldom that I make the rounds. When I do, I feel like a visiting anthropologist, standing aside, detached, as though observing some curious local custom. What fate, I ask myself, would

In wine there is truth.

overtake Martha's Vineyard if a day were to pass without a single cocktail party? Why *do* the parties take place? Does it stand written that certain hours of the day are to be set aside for socializing? Doesn't plenty of that precede the parties — at picnics on the sands of Chappaquiddick or clamming with friends in the mud of Quitsa Pond or batting the breeze with acquaintances one is bound to meet at the post office?

Can it be that, come the late afternoon, a contagion of alcoholic thirst seizes the Island? Perhaps it is an urge to dress up that draws people to parties: More and more, in recent years, ties and coats have come into vogue, even at assemblages in Menemsha and Gay Head, long known as bastions of informality. No doubt, guests look upon their invitations to parties as status symbols — that is, the more invitations they receive, the higher, they imagine, is their social standing. I know of one woman, quite sensible in all other respects, who counts it a sorry day when she isn't asked to more than one party; often she runs into kindred spirits to whom she's just said good-bye. It's a surprising facet of hers, since she is given to discussing serious topics at length, a predilection unlikely to be satisfied at cocktail parties. In fact, it's unusual at them to have a talk of any length about anything. One scarcely has time to greet a fellow guest before someone else materializes. What conversation there is consists of small talk. As it happens, I love small talk, but not at parties, where it's retailed promiscuously. I engage in it only with close friends, for to my way of thinking, small talk is intimate in nature. What a marvelous means of taking one's ease it is to say whatever comes into one's head, no matter how trivial, no matter how silly! But with whom can one do that, except those one knows best?

Whatever the spice of cocktail parties may be, it isn't variety. Lend yourself to the circuit, and you'll find yourself locked into a tight group, condemned to seeing the same old faces, hearing the same old gags, eating the same old olives, exclusive with Alley's, Seward's, and other better shops. If you want to grow weary of even interesting people, see them day in and day out at prescribed hours in a confined setting. Inevitably, as with cocktail circuits elsewhere, everyone's personality stands exposed; our every effort at being charming, our every show of politeness becomes overly familiar and predictable. It's this sameness, I think, that generates an air of cattiness at most large parties. Back in the days when I used to make the scene with fair regularity, I remember that some people were unlovingly dubbed something or other. For example, a lady psychoanalyst, cranky and imperious, was known as The Bitch, even to a coterie of pliant subjects without whom she rarely appeared. Then there was The Caterer, a hulking, watery-eyed man with a gray, fishy pallor who

swam with celebrities by converting his up Island estate into a facility for innumerable entertainments where superior food was to be had. "Here comes The Stewardess," I recall someone once saying at the arrival of a handsome painter of mediocre attainments. She owed her sobriquet to the fact that she wore a perpetual smile. Watching her features encased in a mask of relentless sunshine, I would marvel at the strength of her jaw muscles; my own ache after a few tentative smiles, but then I must have been known as The Stick. I recall, too, groaning inwardly at having to see too much of a nationally famous newscaster whose fame derived from a knack of reciting other people's copy in a voice of easy authority. Confident of his recognizability, he would permit newcomers to the circuit to identify themselves but he would never deign to introduce himself.

My basic beef with the mass rallies I've been talking about is that they're anti-vacation. They're hard work. Think of all the smiles you have to exude. (My friend and neighbor, Walter Werner, thinks they're part sneer, so he calls them "sniles.") Think of the risks you run of being trapped with bores you've been trying to avoid. And then there's the job of "paying back," of producing a mass rally of one's own. Whom to have, whom not to have? Help, help, help! Gradually, one's holiday slips out of control. Summer is pulled out of shape. One

An Edgartown affair

*Part of the up-Island cocktail circuit;
making the rounds*

forgets it's a season for dreaming, not for frantic alertness. Maybe people arriving on the Vineyard for their holiday should be handed punch cards limiting them to a fixed number of parties. If I've sounded curmudgeonly, as I sincerely hope I have, it's because I think that those lucky enough to be on the Vineyard ought to be discerning in how they use their time. The Island's too beautiful to do otherwise. To squander one's few weeks here by being caught up in a merry-go-round of cocktail parties is, I think, a form of desecration. For myself, I'd far rather grow drowsy at home listening to the beat of the whippoorwill's night song.

Daniel Lang makes rare appearances at only the choicest of cocktail parties. He and his wife live in a house that overlooks Menemsha Bight. He has been a war correspondent for The New Yorker *and has written several books. His latest one is called* A Backward Look: Germans Remember.

Maitland Edey coaxes his four wild turkeys.

FOUR WILD TURKEYS
Maitland Edey

Although I have been a bird watcher for more than sixty years, I had never seen a wild turkey until, in astonishment one afternoon, I watched something that resembled a flying mattress go soaring across the North Road just outside of Vineyard Haven and head in the general direction of Lake Tashmoo. I later learned that it was one of a handful that had been introduced to the island by Craig Kingsbury. I saw them again once or twice, but automobiles and dogs were too much for them, and Kingsbury's turkeys disappeared. Later a small flock was established at the Felix Neck sanctuary and has done well there, raising several broods of young.

It was only proper that the wild turkey should be back on the Vineyard after an absence of 150 or 200 years. It is the archetypal New England bird, the symbol of fat fruitful fall bounty. One associates it with the smoky haze of autumn, with Indian summer, with deep drifts of leaves in the woods, with Indians themselves. In Massachusetts the turkey is the avian equivalent of the pumpkin.

Unfortunately, all this is now myth. The turkey lingers here no better than the Indian, its footprints as long gone as the trace of moccasins on the floors of beech and oak glades. What a contrast with the past. When the Pilgrims landed, turkeys were phenomenally abundant, flocks of up to a thousand being encountered. But farming and wild turkeys do not go together. The last one ever seen was shot on Mount Tom near Holyoke in 1851. They shrank away everywhere else too. During my boyhood they were found only in the wilder parts of the Appalachians, in the backwoods of Missouri and Arkansas, and on the coastal islands of the Carolinas and Georgia.

Too bad. Turkeys are magnificent birds. Although they are not as long from tip to tail as pelicans or whistling swans, the two "largest" native eastern North American birds, they have much stouter bodies. For sheer bulk they take the prize. A big tom will weigh in at thirty-five or forty pounds. It can run almost as fast as a dog. For all the exquisite bronzy blues and golds in its plumage, its chestnut tail, its handsome dangling black necktie, and its warty red head, it is a genius at self-effacement. Wary turkeys are almost impossible to find — except at Felix Neck, where they are used to people and hang around the barn like tame birds.

That worries Gus Ben David, the sanctuary's director, who would like to see them re-established as a truly wild population. It was for that reason he decided to give four to me, because I live on a lonely stretch of the North Shore in Chilmark with an abundance of cover and a good supply of natural food. Gus delivered my turkeys on an October morning. He hauled a large wooden crate out of the back of his truck, set it on its side, opened the door, and out went the turkeys like — well, like flying mattresses. They disappeared over some bushes and went zooming down the hill toward the water. Later that day the largest of them, a big tom, was seen down there, gobbling furiously to get his flock together. But they were either too frightened, or else too widely scattered, to respond. Gus had warned me that turkeys are very spooky, that they travel far and fast. I worried that they might have been spooked right out of the area.

To my immense relief I saw two of them a couple of days later, sunning themselves on a hillside near my house and scooping dust into their feathers. I put some cracked corn out there to hold them. The next morning I woke up to find all four of them standing in a row on my deck, staring in through a glass door. From then on there was no problem of tameness, rather one of getting them away from the house, which they appeared to have accepted as a fine substitute for the Felix Neck barn. They trampled down a small rock garden full of maidenhair fern, funchia, and sweet woodruff by pecking at it and snoozing there. We put a wire fence around it; they jumped in over the fence. Even though their daily ration of cracked corn was thrown out several hundred yards from the house, they knew where it came from, and came paddling after me whenever I appeared outside.

This went on for a week. My wife, Helen, and I got to know them well. There was Big George, the adult tom; there was George's Girlfriend, an adult hen; there was the Teen-age Dropout, an adolescent boy turkey (whose name was not quite fair to him, for all four were generous droppers-out of material we preferred not to find on our deck); and finally there was the Scruffy Kid, an extremely rumpled little-girl turkey about one sixth the size of Big George.

Their pecking order was very strong. Big George was the leader. Where he went the others followed. If they got in his way he pecked at them and they jumped smartly. Girlfriend pecked the other two, and the Scruffy Kid pecked nobody. The corn I fed them was only a small part of their diet. They ate leaves, grass, weed seeds, and were extraordinarily quick at chasing and snatching any late moths or grasshoppers that they put up during their incessant patrolling of the woods and bushes around the house. Every morning when we got up they were on the lawn cropping grass.

One morning they weren't. They were absent all day and all the next. Late in the afternoon we took a walk through all the paths and cover within half a mile of our house. Finally, on the beach we found

Gus Ben David,
proprietor of Felix Neck sanctuary, poses
with his favorite fine feathered friend,
"Hoot."

Big George's footprints, enormous marks in the sand. But mixed in with them were the prints of a barefoot man and apparently those of a very small dog. Had Big George, big innocent hungry George, allowed himself to be approached and grabbed? Was twenty-five pounds of dressed turkey now resting in someone's freezer? We went home extremely distressed.

The following afternoon, Election Day, we got word that the turkeys had been seen on the North Road. After voting, we drove home very slowly, scanning the bushes on either side. Suddenly there they were. And there were Messrs. Dunham and Daub, two men who lived nearby, giving them some corn.

"Thank God, our turkeys," I said.

"Yours? We didn't know where they came from. We're trying to lure them away from the road and get them mixed in with our guinea hens. They're sure to get killed if they hang around here."

That was certainly so. Passing motorists skidded to a stop only when they saw us standing there and the turkeys strolling back and forth.

"Where do you live?" asked Mr. Daub.

"Near the water, about a mile and a half from here."

"Can you catch them?"

"Not possibly."

"Can you herd them home?"

"No way. Turkeys can't be herded."

"You'll have to lead them, then."

He gave me his can of corn. When Big George had polished off what was lying on the ground, I gave the can a shake to get his attention and dribbled a few grains in the grass. He came bounding over and ate them. I moved off about fifty feet and dribbled again. He followed; so did the others. Feeling like the Pied Piper, I dribbled corn across a field and up a wood path, doling out grains in increasingly small amounts because I didn't want the turkeys to get so full that they would lose interest. We finally hit the dirt road that runs in to my house. The turkeys were now pelting along at a good clip. I had to walk backward, keeping a constant eye on them, because if they got too close they stopped, and if I got too far ahead they would also stop and begin eating things along the edge of the road. Also it was beginning to get dark and I was afraid that they would suddenly fly off and roost somewhere.

"Don't make them go so fast," called Helen, "they'll get tired."

"Tired! You try walking backward for a couple of miles."

It got darker. The turkeys waddled along like gnomes. Just at nightfall we arrived at home. I threw some corn on the hill and was immensely relieved to find the birds there the next morning.

That was two weeks ago. The turkeys are as tame as ever, and now seem strongly bound to this place as their home base. I don't know what frightened them away. It may have been that man and his dog on the beach. Now, however, I think they are settled here. They know the area well, and if they are spooked again they will probably find their way back. They roost at night in trees somewhere very close by — I haven't found that place yet, and won't disturb them by looking for it. Meanwhile, I put out less and less corn. Yesterday twenty quail found it, and they were running between the legs of the turkeys like mice, the bigger birds seeming to be ostrich-sized by comparison. Today the turkeys were gone for four or five hours. They are beginning to manage on their own.

I am leaving the island in December and won't be back until April. I hope they get through the winter, that no hunter shoots them, that dogs don't harass them, that they find the corn that will be put out on their hill once a week while we are gone. In April I hope to see them again, just a shadow of them feeding at daybreak — as wild birds, tame no longer.

UPDATE — The turkeys survived their first winter, but on the island of Chappaquiddick. My neighbors did not like the way the turkeys ate their bird seeds and trampled their flower beds and soiled their porches. They had to be trapped and moved.

Oh dear

Maitland Edey is the former managing editor of
Time-Life Books *and has recently retired to live on
the North Shore of the Vineyard to devote his full
time to writing. His previous eight books deal with
natural history or zoological subjects. His most
recent is a thoughtful and informative commentary
to* Great Photographic Essays from Life *(1978).
He is currently finishing a book about early
hominid evolution in collaboration with
paleoanthropologist Donald Johanson.*

Bordering pines at the Martha's Vineyard State Forest

Stranded

WINTER SUITE
Phyllis Méras

It is a slate-gray day today. Fall is ending and it is the edge of winter. Two weeks ago, I picked bittersweet on the West Chop road, and crimson sumac at Indian Hill. There were still leaves swirling and chasing each other — bronze racing brown. And there were splashes of huckleberry, like the sumac — a royal red in the West Tisbury woods.

I keep a haphazard nature notebook and I see that my entry for last Saturday says, "Red-gold morning; a woodpecker is pecking. Some leaves are almond-blond; a handful still a paling green. There is lavender wild aster here and there in up-Island fields."

Today there is only occasional crimson; no lavender. The only gold I see is a wild rosebush in a sheltered place, and in the woods it is brown — brown leaves crackle beneath my feet; brown pine needles make a smooth carpet. Now and again, green moss patches climb a damp bank, but like the red of crimson and huckleberry, the green is occasional.

Along the Lambert's Cove road, the stone walls that are hidden in summertime by foliage and flowers wriggle like dinosaurs' backbones over the fields.

I am not fond of fall. It is an end, not a beginning. It is the time for boarding up houses, pulling up boats, raking dead leaves, putting up all the pleasurable things of summer. As long as I can remember, I have wanted fall to pass quickly. I admire it surely, for the crispness of its air, the crispness of its colors, but I find it discomfiting.

Winter, on the other hand — especially an Island winter — is magical. The landscape extends. Roads that used to have a beginning and an end, fields that had bounds, no longer seem to. All blend into one another. Even the ponds, iced over if winter is cold enough, extend the landscape.

When I was a child, and only a summer visitor to the Vineyard, there was no excitement grander than the prospect of an Island Christmas. Of course, it meant nights spent on cots in a cold East Chop summer house with the kerosene smells from a space heater making eyes smart and hair and clothes smell acrid, but then morning would come, and outside the house there were white woods and silence.

I have never lost that childhood affection for winter. I like walking winter beaches when there are rare discoveries to be made — cedar planks on the Gay Head shore, salt-bleached gnarled driftwood. Though there are no flowers in winter, if a snowfall has been heavy enough, there are sure to be snow blossoms — great bouquets of white in the crotches of trees.

In the Oak Bluffs Camp Ground, snow rests in the gingerbread cutouts of the cottages and frosts their peaks. Edgartown's big white houses look more imposing than at any other season.

There is a cosiness in winter — a nestling up —

Slim pickings during the winter at Sweetened Water Farm

Signs of Christmas in Vineyard Haven

invitations to hot tea or hot glogg after snow walks; a striking up of conversations with passers-by; an eagerness to share the beauty; to exchange news of winter birds passing through — chartreuse evening grosbeaks, purple finches. There is talk of the scallop beds. Are the Cape Poge Pond scallops as abundant this year as last?

At Christmastime, there is a welcome busyness. Primitive Mexican crèches in the window at Tashtego; sophisticated Old World baubles on a silvered tree at Alan-Mayhew Ltd. Santa Claus riding the fire engine in Vineyard Haven and Edgartown causes a great stir.

The West Tisbury Congregational Church tower is illumined against the black-velvet nighttime sky. In Edgartown, the carols are played. Of course, it is somewhat the same in any small community off-Island, but I have lived in those, too, and there is a special comradeship to a Vineyard Christmas, born,

Winter can have its highlights.

I suspect, of insularity.

If you walk in the woods just after a fresh snow-fall, there is the mystery — and the companionship — of animal tracks. Are they the hops of a rabbit that kicks up the snow? Or are they the tracks of a feral cat able to fend and forage in fall, stalking in cold and hunger now that winter has come?

I explored the Indian Hill woods one snowy morning last winter. I headed alone for the North Shore. The fresh snow squeaked under my black boots. The rocks in the brooks, sheathed in ice, glittered like giant diamonds. Here and there, stream water had frozen as it tumbled. I walked and admired, and remembered other winters — other places — the way one does alone in the snow.

I remembered watching the waves thud along the Katama shore, and the flume fly and a cold, hard snow bite my cheeks and sting my eyelids when I thought I would venture out one near-blizzard afternoon to see what the Atlantic Ocean was doing.

Looking out, I recalled how, when I was small, my father, nodding and pointing into the distance, had told me how Spain was "just over there" and I had believed him. And I thought, too, of a snowfall the first time I had crossed that ocean and was sitting on a park bench in Switzerland by the River Rhone, watching the snowflakes melting on the sleek feathers of the black water birds.

And they, in turn, reminded me of the crows that came every morning when we lived in the West Tisbury parsonage, and cawed ceaselessly till they were fed — till the bread crusts and eggshells of breakfast had been put out on the snow for them. Then they would swoop down from the big oak tree by the barn, fly up from the Mill Pond, and hop about on the snow, flapping black wings. And when they were done, back they would go to the oak tree limbs and sit for a while like witches' familiars.

A favorite pond for skating,
West Tisbury

The Islander *breaks through the ice
in the dead of winter.*

*Snowstorm on Circuit Avenue
in Oak Bluffs*

I remembered walking to school in a New Hampshire winter, up over a hill, across a field where, in spring, the first wild strawberries bloomed and the bluets peeked. In winter, the hillside was given over to sledders, so I always longed for the school day to be over so I could quit the sepulchral beige halls with their plaster-cast busts of Augustus and Julius Caesar, and swoop down the hill on a sled.

But the reverie ended, for suddenly, there in the Indian Hill woods, a mastiff stood — quite as startled as I. He stood his ground. I stood mine. We were on the same path, heading opposite ways. I had spent the winter at Indian Hill, but we had never met before. And we never met again. After each of us took the measure of the other we cautiously passed. He was not a friendly, tail-wagging dog. He was a dog intent on the hunt, and he did not wish to be disturbed.

When I got to the water, there were deer tracks in a flurry in the snow and I wondered if the dog and the deer had met, and if they had, how the deer had made its escape. I have read, of course, how sometimes they swim. And I looked out over the water, but seagulls on rocks and a few scoters were the only signs of life.

I ambled along the beach for a while. I was looking for driftwood that might make a mantel. But what there was, of course, was frozen too hard among the rocks and the snow to dislodge.

So I made my way back, up through Cedar Tree Neck, looking for animal tracks again and smelling wood smoke from inviting chimneys.

I am looking forward to winter, but now it is barely the end of October. I have a while to wait.

Phyllis Méras is a contributing editor of the Vineyard Gazette, *as well as travel editor for the* Providence Journal *and editor of the Wellesley College alumnae magazine. Phyllis is the author of many books, mostly dealing with how-to subjects, her most recent being* Christmas Angels. *She lives in Vineyard Haven but commutes to Providence. She may be the most peripatetic of Vineyarders, and the most devoted to her Island home.*

Snow blossoms cling to branches and a stone wall in Gay Head.

Saltwater ice freezes to Squibnocket rocks
on a zero day in February.

THANKSGIVING WALK
Rose Styron

A Vineyard place
of undeciphered signs. The road stands still,
widens among the flints and copper ferns
and climbs
a grass-abandoned hill.

Oakleaves rustle underfoot, charged,
wary of rain.
November's sun, sly laser, streaks a field
drowsing to Indian glory as if done
with the nourishment of grain.

Savannah sparrows in the empty furrow play
hopscotch. A southern tune.
Red squirrels from my childhood leap the air.
A crow is king in the peeling sycamore.

The clarion loon turns every wind-belled charm
toward golden dangers:
a fall from limbs of grace; release; be found
as leaves brighter than autumn jewelry floating
the walls, sands, buoys of Vineyard Sound.

I have been afraid to lose my way, desire
magic of summer, the extending light,
afraid of scholarship, looking too close
or down each traitor height.

Or poised to follow where the snow moon sailed
I'd court its misty brilliance till the true
moon stared back, beckoned. Then I'd deny
the night's wit and the stars'
laughter, the sweet tide. Rue, rue.

Yet certain now my unpaced footsteps skim
somewhere the familiar ledge,
old fears of plunging disengaged, gone
in an afternoon allegro,
the rayed edge

of clouds. Sunset will come, and winter
but through the always anguished-and-too-early dark
I sense they scheme
to haunt no longer all my Chilmark sanctuaries,
only illuminate

those manuscripts, this harvest-buried dream.

Born in Baltimore (of all places), Rose Styron attended Wellesley College. She soon married William Styron. She has had two volumes of poetry published, From Summer to Summer *(for children), and* A Thieves' Afternoon. *She is the mother of four, a hostess of renown, a translator and a writer of articles for such periodicals as the* Nation, *the* New Republic *and* Ms. *If she has any weakness, it is her backhand, a quality exploited with some relish by other contributors to this book.*

Quansoo Road on Thanksgiving

The North Tisbury oak tree

A December rain coats a Washington Thorn Tree in Vineyard Haven.

The years go by on a Felix Neck rooftop.

Menemsha postcard

REPRISE

Nicholas Delbanco

I had been away for years, making an inland home. And the last time I returned was in early April; it rained the three days of my stay. Fog hovered; the Island felt sluiced down and chill. This made no difference, of course; to the passionate pilgrim all weather signifies, all skies are metaphoric. So I drove the roads, from Vineyard Haven to Gay Head, with the kind of body knowledge that takes no note of time. Each curve felt familiar, and I shifted gears where first I'd learned to shift them fifteen years before. The lanes and gulleys and bluffs seemed the same; the sea attested to consistency in change. Even the garbage dump seemed an occasion for nostalgia; I took South Road, then Middle Road, then North Road, ratifying that the sand and trees remained. . . .

Sooner or later one asks oneself why — what is it in *this* arrangement of space that signifies so deeply, why *this* place and no other place should so retain its hold? I pretend it doesn't. I say you can't go home again, I say it's built up and too touristy, the shopping takes too long. The Wellfleet beaches are wider and open to all, the Indian Ocean is finer for swimming, the cliffs at Dover are more impressive, and the taste and price of lobster are better in Dingwall Bay. I mention the Cyclades and the Grenadines and Bali; I tell anyone who'll listen how I'm through with all such nonsense, the young man's dream of freedom from a gilded shingled cage.

It doesn't work. It's fraud. It's useless to pretend, no matter how faithless and far-off I've been, that there's any other landscape I could learn to love. It's as if some philter had been slipped in my first cup of coffee on my first trip on the *Islander,* and I've been helplessly an addict since. I'd know that doughnut anywhere, the pitch and yaw of coffee in its cup like a miniature ocean, the smoke-wreathed face above. Perhaps the great minds of our century can see a continent as island, knowing the four sea walls of North America and claiming the whole turf between. But the four sea walls of the Vineyard are the limits of my easy ranging, and what follows is an exile's piece of praise.

I worked for Poole's Fish Market, and used to

Dutcher Dock catch.

*The untarnished image
of summer.*

drive the truck. Once I dropped a three-hundred-pound swordfish on the Main Street of Vineyard Haven, accelerating. Three fish were destined for the ferry, and I'd left the tailgate down. I dropped a bushel of quahaugs, also, on the Main Street of Oak Bluffs, but that wasn't as satisfying — the explosion was muted by comparison, a sequence of pops, and the crowd took cover instead of crowding around. I'd drive for hours daily, making trip after trip till the Island seemed endless and each delivery or dropoff point an illusion: where do such circles start?

And so it is with memory; the process seems wreathed to itself. Select one single skein and see how the others are linked. Everything seems circular, a concentric circle round the pattern that the spear grass makes, inscribing its circumference with wind. I cannot think of friendship, love, or isolation without thinking of the Island, those times as well as that space, cannot think of spring without the winter there.

We each have our grab bag of touchstones, our untarnished images. The way the dew feels in the early mornings, for instance, or the dunes at Zack's Cliffs fading from view, accumulating, in a heat haze an hour's walk distant. The boys with drop lines hunting squid, a friend who used to fish by lying on the beach and waiting for the gulls to swoop, then racing pell-mell to cast at that spot. The old abandoned Brick Works and King's Highway overgrown; the density of salt-sea air and what it does to rising bread; the farm where horses nuzzle, nudging at stone walls. The clatter and chatter of boats in their berths, the way the sunset could ignite the windows of the houses in the dark hills opposite, feeding them chill flame. An osprey over Noman's Land; the long-haired lady steering a sunfish, with maybe a poodle on board; a sky so thick with stars the nearest seemed near-palpable, Sunday morning baseball games, Wednesday evening poker, the Saturday afternoon sailboat races on Quitsa Pond, the place the great blue herons nest, bloody marys and fried chicken and *sashimi* on the beach, a Siren with guitar at work

And the race is on at Chilmark Pond.

Dr. Milton Mazer scrutinizes the results.

A soft summer rain

on chord progressions, her lower lip sucked in —
that intensely earnest sense of self that heralds first
prowess, and joy. I think of cocktail parties, tupelo
trees, the tennis courts at last light, or the
lobstermen leaving by dawn — call it nostalgia,
islomania, call it a passionate addiction or the
license of sunshot and soft-focus memory. Call it,
more simply, love.

I should not like to close without one tribute to
one name. There are many friends one wants to list
— but, for me, Max Eastman remains the Island's
mage. We were nearly sixty years apart, yet I can
count on the fingers of a single maimed hand the
men who have meant more to me, or to whom I've
felt as close. Max was generosity incarnate in his
eighties, and I remember staying with him one
October. Yvette was off to New York for a shopping
trip, and she asked me to stay in their place in Gay
Head: a favor to me, really, since my own hut was
unheated. I was full of beans and bravado then, and
would get to work by six — waking up and clacking
at the keys in my upstairs bedroom. In the first
pause, however, I could hear his steady hunt-and-
peck in the study underneath; he'd been at work
well before. So we'd share a cup of coffee and a
comment on the news, then I'd fuss at my novel
again. At nine o'clock or so I'd take a break — tear
off my clothes and run down the hill to the pond.
The morning would be glorious: that crystalline
light, those sizable skies, the pine trees somehow
greener against the sere scrub oak. And always, out
there from the still warm water, Max would lift his
hand to me, his white mane on the wavelets like
some snowy egret's, grinning.

Things change. He died; I married a girl from
America — the place that begins with Woods Hole.
And I've not been back much, since. But it takes no
effort to see this again, see it always as the spirit's
emblem: an old man waving from the water at the
youth on the near shore. They are naked, both of
them; the sun slants over Lobsterville. A few day
sailors might be on the pond, or someone in a
kayak, or musseling or digging clams. The seabirds
settle, incurious; the beach smells of seawrack and
tide. There's a busy imitation of silence: The man in
the water, bobbing, flutters heels and hands. The
young one runs to meet him and it's all a perfect
clarity until he does a surface dive and, splashing,
shuts his eyes.

Max Eastman, 1945.

*Although he is no longer an annual Vineyard
resident, Nicholas Delbanco's Island roots are
deep. He spent his formative years in a small
camp perched high atop a Chilmark bluff where he
wrote and cavorted. He is the author of nine
novels, one of which,* Consider Sappho Burning,
*takes place on the Vineyard. His most recent book
is called* Sherbrookes, *and the final volume of his
Vermont trilogy,* Stillness, *will appear this fall.
Currently, Nicholas lives in Bennington, Vermont,
and is a professor at a well-known college nearby.
For some obscure reason, he now summers on
the Cape.*

NOT FOR EVERYBODY, THANK GOD!!

Ruth Gordon

Morning glories, white picket fence, and boat, Edgartown mainstays

Edgartown! It's where it started. I mean it's where *I* started talking. According to my mother, an Episcopalian but often telling a whopper, I said "Papa" and "Mama" before any other known or unknown baby. Then in Edgartown, where great talkers Daniel Webster and Nathaniel Hawthorne put up at the Edgartown Inn and talker Clare Boothe Luce stayed at the Daggett House, at the Teller House in 1898, Ruth Gordon Jones — that's me — said to the waitress, when offered a skimpy slice of cantaloupe, "When I'm home I have much." My first whole sentence. Maybe if you can't think of anything to say, come to Edgartown, see what it does for *you.*

For brains, there's Vineyard Haven. That's where Lillian Hellman uses hers, any John Hersey, and William Styron.

If you're looking for class — Chilmark; or over the other side of the Island where Kay Graham knows enough to leave Washington and has a house with a lot of land with a lot of trees and arriving Air New England or departing is everybody you see or hear about, her weekend guests.

Down at Lake Tashmoo is Jimmy Cagney on his boat. André Previn, leaving his orchestra in London, is living in his and wife Mia Farrow's house. On TV, André is in white tie and tails, but on Main Street, Vineyard Haven, he's buying more shorts and sweatshirts from Brickman's. And Mia and their five children arrive after making a movie on the Nile, and after making a movie on Bora. They like it fine.

"Oh Ruthie," wrote Mia one winter when we weren't here, "if you could *see* the snow falling on the driftwood."

Mia has a sense of what's what.

Back in the woods back of Tashmoo live Carly Simon and James Taylor.

Up Gay Head way is great if you like red cliffs and the open sea way down below. Indians live up here and Jackie Onassis is going to. She's bought a great three hundred and something acres.

When I was little, the Indians had oxen that pulled things. The only other oxen I ever saw pulling stuff were at St. Tropez. That's nice, too, but no Edgartown or Gay Head or Chilmark or Vineyard Haven or West Tisbury, which I wouldn't know *how* to describe. It's all over everywhere. Wherever you don't know where you are it's West Tisbury.

St. Tropez had a nightingale and I never saw one here, but we have some loud woodpeckers and bobwhites and Baltimore orioles and at my house a squirrel I wish was in St. Tropez. He runs up my

Edgartown Harbor

sunflowers and bends them over like giant croquet wickets, then eats all the sunflower seeds. My sunflowers grow fourteen feet tall and look better up straight than hooped over, but in any position they're my favorite flower and I wish that squirrel would leave Cottage Street and work his way into our Edgartown Market where they have got a fine selection of everything to offer, including red and white wine made on the Vineyard, which is expensive but worth it.

Coming, going, parked, you see cars with New York plates, and Arkansas and Texas and Maine, New Hampshire, Vermont, Ontario — a lot from California, Minnesota, Pennsylvania, Connecticut, Massachusetts, Mississippi — what's so different here?

What's so different, here you change the rhythm. The Island of Martha's Vineyard has its own, and a great way to tone up is to change your rhythm.

Always there's an exception and here he's Henry Beetle Hough, who lives here all the time and only goes off Island to receive a degree from Columbia University or meet with the Thoreau Society. He's going on eighty-two and you can wish you had a face like his. Wrinkles? Not a . . . and is in there writing for our newspaper, fighting for our salt marshes, and what *he* does to change his rhythm, write and ask him, care of the *Vineyard Gazette,* Edgartown, Massachusetts 02539.

Well, what can I tell you? We *did* have an Indian they said was named Charlie Medicine but I don't see him around anymore so he may have joined the majority.

Henry Beetle Hough
outside the Gazette *office*

Ruth Gordon is a permanent transient living on Cottage Street in Edgartown. Her most recent films are Every Which Way but Loose *and* Boardwalk. *Her* An Open Book *tells about some others.*

Typical quaintness of an Edgartown abode

Edgartown Harbor,
as seen through a wire fence

*A morning walk past the Town Hall
and movie theater*

The path to Tashmoo Farm.

*A small-pond reflection behind
the Dr. Daniel Fisher house*

Still life window.

TO THE MEASURE OF MAN

Garson Kanin

Somerset Maugham, asked to describe life on Martha's Vineyard, declared, "Well, there's *ebsolutely* nothing to do and *ebsolutely* no time to do it!"

Many of us find it so. Seeking an escape from the dreaded twin enemies of creativity — interruption and distraction — we find ourselves constantly interrupted here by beauty and often distracted by peace.

The better part of my life is spent on two islands: Martha's Vineyard and Manhattan. It is difficult to believe that the former is four times as large as the latter. But so it is. There are, however, more significant differences. The immortal Leonardo admired still another island, Venice, because, he observed, "It is the last city on earth built to the measure of man." Alas, he never saw *our* island which, although hardly a city, merits his description.

Manhattan, for all its splendors and wonders, reduces us by means of relativity to the size of insects in both body and spirit. The Vineyard,

An intimate Chilmark shed.

conversely, places us again in proper perspective to the nature of the surrounding atmosphere, restoring our battered human dignity.

Manhattan takes my breath away. The Vineyard gives it back.

But even the most myopically optimistic among us have begun to perceive that there is trouble in paradise. We form a microcosm of the societal pattern: a struggle between the selfish and the unselfish; between those who have some concern for those yet to come and those whose God is the expediency of the moment; between the civilized who would preserve for the many and the predatory who would profit for the few.

At times, the clean, bracing air fairly tingles with tension. The battle is joined. Who will *win* the war? As with all wars — no one. Damage will be done, some of it irreparable. Yet it is vital to pursue a delaying action.

The balladeer sings: "The times they are a' changin'...." and of course they should and they must. The question is: Changin' for what? For better? Or worse?

Some years ago, before my wife and I settled here, we lucked out on a rental. The owners of one of the Island's most elegant homes kindly consented to let us have it for a month while they traveled abroad. On the day we moved in, the redoubtable Ed Tyra was there to welcome us. He showed us about, explained the equipment. As he made ready to leave, I said, "Oh. Just one thing more."

"Yes?"

"The keys."

"The keys?" he echoed dubiously, as though I had requested the combination to the vault of the Edgartown National Bank.

"Yes," I repeated. "The keys. To the front door? And the back door?" He was regarding me curiously. I began to feel like a character in *Alice in Wonderland*. "So we can lock the house," I said. "When we go out."

"Oh," said Ed, troubled. "The keys. Yes. I believe there *once* used to be some. The people who owned the house before — or maybe it was the ones before *them.* I'll look around in the cellar — try to find them for you." He exuded an air of no confidence whatever.

I was well and truly bewildered. "But wasn't the house locked just now — before we arrived?" I insisted. "It *must* have been — all these beautiful, valuable things."

"Why, no," Ed replied. "We never lock our houses around here. What would be the point? Hell, my wife and I went to Florida for three months last winter and we didn't lock *our* house."

In time, the keys were found, but when in Rome — or when in Edgartown . . . we found that we did

*Vineyarders know how
to beat the system.*

*Summer tourism; the struggle between
selfish and unselfish*

*Lunch break
at the old Mister C's
in Oak Bluffs.*

not lock up, either.

A passage of time.

Now, many houses here are equipped with complex and sophisticated (and expensive) alarm systems, double locks, triple locks, bars, electrical devices, dogs. Prudent summer residents carefully select reliable house-sitters for the winter season.

What happened? Apparently the seven miles of water separating us from the mainland were not enough to immunize the Island against the current social poisons, the contemporary diseases. We have begun to be plagued with our proportionate share of lawbreaking and drugs and permissive nonsense and assaults and juvenile criminals and breaking-and-entering and even unspeakable rape.

Fortunately, the Island is proving to be an unhappy incubus for noisemakers, litterers, slobs, common nuisances, trespassers, pushers, scofflaws, and fuckups. The ambience is simply too simple, intimate, integrated, personal — thus not conducive to getting away with it. This is comforting to those of us who cherish the land and sea and green and brooks and beaches and paths and shelters and ponds and secret places and bridges and the myriad old old structures that are charming continua, gracefully recalling a treasured past, gravely heralding a hopeful future, and calmly lending a sense of forever. Above all we are caught by the magic that all these in concert generate.

In time I suppose the Island will go the way of the world. I am grateful that I shall not be around to see it in its altered form.

Although I was born many many miles from here, I feel like an Islander — at least I felt like an Islander until just the other night.

Our dinner guests are a dear Island couple (Quahog chowder, female chicken lobsters from Poole's, corn from Fred Fisher's farm, salad from the garden reinforced with fresh herbs from Greene's, lemon meringue pie, chilled Chicama Chardonnay). The wife of the pair is a descendant of one of the Island's oldest families. The husband was brought here in a basket by his parents when he was eighteen months old. He is now eighty and except for his college years, has spent his lifetime living and doing business on the Island.

In the course of the evening's conversation, I ask him a question having to do with Island history and custom.

"Oh!" says the wife. "Don't ask *him* stuff like that. *He* wouldn't know."

"Why not?"

"Why, because," she says with esoteric logic, "he's an off-Islander!"

Ah well.

Still, what matters in the end is not Islander or off-Islander, but Island. Beloved Island.

Rosebud.

Garson Kanin, author of the best-selling Moviola,
is also a playwright (Born Yesterday), *novelist*
(A Thousand Summers; One Hell of an Actor),
memoirist (Tracy and Hepburn; Remembering
Mr. Maugham), *stage director* (The Diary of Anne
Frank; Funny Girl; Fledermaus), *film director* (A
Man to Remember; The Great Man Votes; Bachelor
Mother; My Favorite Wife; They Knew What They
Wanted; Tom, Dick and Harry; Some Kind of a Nut;
Where It's At; The True Glory), *screenwriter* (It
Should Happen to You; Adam's Rib; Pat and Mike;
A Double Life; The Marrying Kind) *and recently,
crusader (*It Takes a Long Time to Become Young).
He is married to Ruth Gordon.

*Ruth Gordon and Garson Kanin enjoy their
little summer retreat on Cottage Street
in Edgartown.*

Quitsa Pond reflections of a still evening.

LOBSTERVILLE,
CHILDHOOD, AND SUMMER DAYS
Dionis Coffin Riggs

As soon as school closed my playmate, Grace, moved with her family to Lobsterville. I was invited to spend a week with her before the summer was over.

The problem of my getting there was solved by Mr. Gifford, who told my grandmother I might ride up to Menemsha in the order cart when Fred made one of his semiweekly trips for the store. Fred was not in a position to protest at having a nine-year-old for company, so early one Thursday morning he stopped for me on his way to his job. I waited on the store steps, sitting on the breadbox, while he hitched the horse to a wagon that looked like a miniature prairie schooner. It was supplied with dry goods and groceries that Fred was to deliver in Chilmark.

The day was warm, but the canvas hood of the wagon sheltered us. The leisurely pace of the horse made a pleasant breeze where the roadbed was reasonably hard. When the wheels were slowed down by sand, we were hot.

We turned into every lane, every driveway, every farmyard, and there were many farms in Chilmark in those days. Dogs barked at the sound of hoofs and wheels, but when they saw the familiar wagon they came up to us, wagging their tails.

At each house Fred took in groceries, and after an interminable time, he came out with a page of his order-book filled, and his pencil over his ear.

HALFWAY AND HUNGRY

By noon we were only halfway there, and I was hungry. Lots of good food was stowed away in that wagon, but Fred didn't offer me any, nor did he take anything for himself.

At last he turned into a lane leading toward the South Shore. I could hear the regular beat of the surf, and the air was cool. Wild roses were still in bloom, and meadow larks were singing. When we stopped in a barnyard Fred took out oats for the horse and put a bag of them under its nose.

In the house no word was spoken, but Fred signaled, and another place was added to those already set at a big table. All during the meal we could hear the steady hum of surf, and intermittent sounds of chewing. No one spoke except Fred, who occasionally made some remark in a deadpan way about his host and hostess. It puzzled and worried me. But the food was delicious. Not until we were on our way again did Fred tell me the couple were deaf and dumb.

In the late afternoon we arrived at Menemsha where Grace, her parents, and older brothers were waiting. They had finished the weekly errands and were eager to take advantage of the outgoing tide.

Grace and I sat in the bow of the big catboat with

Childhood daffodils.

Menemsha

spray splashing our bare feet, and wind blowing our Dutch-cut hair.

There used to be a long wharf at Lobsterville, but in those days it had deteriorated so much it was never used. We were not allowed even to walk out on it. The catboat was moored in front of the houses, and we were rowed ashore.

Two rows of tiny houses (about a dozen), like Camp Ground cottages, were strung along the shore with boardwalks connecting each house. The two rows were held together by another walk that crossed the sand between the two rows. Grace's house was the easternmost, on the second row.

Fish chowder was ready, and places set on the oilcloth-covered table. With apple pie from the bakery at Menemsha, it was a delicious supper.

When we finished, Grace took me around to visit the neighbors, all interested in the newcomer. At that time only one other child lived there: a little boy named Onslow, who lived with his

grandparents. They had a hammock on the porch where we spent hours, pretending we were in a boat, or counting vessels as they passed through Vineyard Sound. Sometimes as many as a hundred sailed or steamed by in an hour.

Each morning the fishermen went out to haul their lobster pots. We could hear their motors in the early morning while we were still in bed.

Back in the hills we found a pond with lilies opened wide in the sun. We had to dodge the poison ivy that lined the path.

On Sunday we walked up a steep hill, past Ryan's, and over to the South Side to the Gay Head church. The ocean sounded very close, an accompaniment for the hymns and the sermon.

MUSSELS ROASTED IN SEAWEED

Grace's brother promised us a great treat if we would get mussels from the old wharf spiles. He

Gay Head patterns

The Gay Head lighthouse welcomes travelers by road and sea.

made a driftwood fire that evening and roasted mussels on seaweed. In the night we woke and saw the coast guardsman walking past, flashing a thin beam with his lantern.

Grace would have no girls to play with when I left. Her family urged me to stay longer. But my mother and sisters were back in West Tisbury for their summer vacations, and I had been away a long time. They had arranged for me to come back with Cousin Dan, who had an automobile, and would be going home from Menemsha.

Probably it was the automobile that changed Lobsterville. The fishermen's families no longer found it necessary to live in isolation. It was a pleasant, neighborly way of life, an unforgettable place to visit.

Dionis Coffin Riggs is now in her early eighties. She was born in Edgartown from a family of whaling captains. After the death of her father, she lived in Brooklyn, New York, but was always back "on Island" for the summer. In 1940 she wrote a best-selling biography of her grandmother, From off Island, *and has been writing ever since. A collection of her poetry was published in 1969:* Sea Born Island. *She also collaborated with three other Vineyard poets for a collection called* Martha's Vineyard. *She continues to be published in the* Vineyard Gazette *and the* Christian Science Monitor. *Recently she completed an endurance walk benefiting a local charity. It is safe to say that people one-third her age fell by the wayside as this octogenarian Yankee plodded on — no doubt writing poems in her mind as she trekked the long course. Dionis lives year-round in West Tisbury.*

Poised for fishing off Gay Head and Menemsha.

Wheels of yesteryear on the Hancock Farm

Windy Gates lot

PROCREATIONS
Stanley Burnshaw

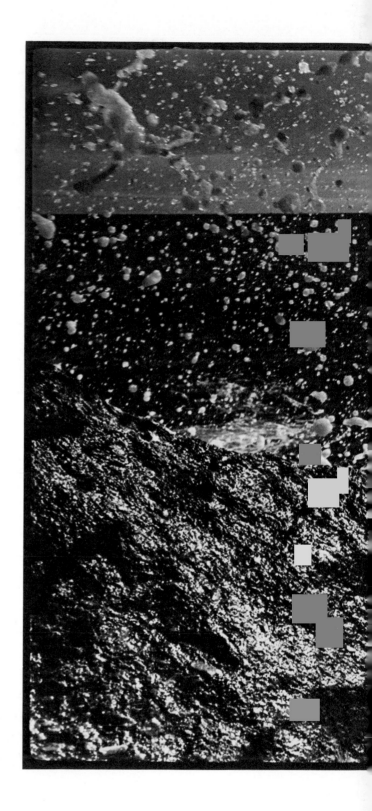

... and yet and everywhere
Wreaths are curling up from the sand:
The sea's salt with the leaf's land
   In a fuse of air:
Bursts of streaming shape and sound,
Twining creations of soil and mist —

   Watching near and far
To draw from the ever-unfolding swarm
   Sparks of bestowing form,
And failing at our own command,
We weary towers out of a cave,
Forcing upon the inviolate ground
   Our witness stones ...

   And will this need desist
   When coming nothing stands,
When the rock rises against the wave
   With taking hands?

*Stanley Burnshaw was born in New York City in
1906. He is the author of twelve books, including*
The Seamless Web, The Poem Itself, *and* In the
Terrified Radiance, *from which this piece is
excerpted. A distinguished man of letters, his book*
The Seamless Web *has received international
attention. He lives with his wife on Lambert's Cove
and when not in his study writing he can be found
gardening, his favorite pastime.*

Gay Head

A Gay Head stroll in mist

INTO THE FUTURE DARKLY
Henry Beetle Hough

I met Eli Ginzberg one day at Chappaquansett, and he put to me the question, "Has the decline of the Vineyard been more rapid than you expected, or less rapid?"

"Oh," I said, "much more rapid."

"It's been much less rapid than I expected," he said. "That's the difference between an environmentalist and an economist."

No difference about what had been happening, only the question of how fast the decline.

Twice lately I have heard a newcomer to the Island exclaim about the extent of open space here, and each one has asked the same question in almost the same words: "Why hasn't it been built up?" I could only reply by invoking what the questioner obviously thought exceptional, unlikely, transitory, and most of all irrelevant to the present times.

And the questioner was the realist. One may discern the certainty that some enclaves of open space will be preserved on the Island here and there, but no possibility that this natural resource of an unspoiled Island can outlast the next few years. Preservation has become the function of interested groups or philanthropists or the desire of the wealthy, and in the face of continually rising real-estate values one can only view this phase as limited and precarious.

The happy combination of hill, declivity and plain, extensive regions and vistas of moor, pond, oak woods, windblown copses; of marsh ready to flame in fall color; of high bluffs and broad, sandy beaches; of boulders, old dirt roads; of memory, legend, and history, is doomed by overwhelming forces.

Why is this so?

Inflation progresses hand in hand with the irresistible increase in real-estate values. Examples come with the force of an avalanche. Two hundred acres in West Tisbury that were sold a decade previously for $1.00 an acre exchanged hands in 1972 for $20,000 and were resold within six months for $232,000. This is the pattern. There will be breathing spells, but each wave will be followed by another and then another. There is only so much Island land, and the demand will not be satisfied.

Each sale, no matter how tinged with the speculative notions of "developers," automatically increases the taxable value of abutting and neighboring property, adding to the burden of the owners and at the same time opening opportunities for them to sell for large profits.

And here comes the Supreme Judicial Court of Massachusetts to rule that all real estate must be assessed at "full and fair market value." In the consequent escalation of assessments, open land suffers most. Most of it, held — often for generations — by families of moderate means, will be subdivided and sold out of the sheer necessity of the owners.

Those who hope to keep large properties intact must take steps to meet the exactions of the Internal Revenue Service when death requires a transfer of ownership to a new generation. The conservation easement is recommended as a practical recourse in estate planning. When land is stripped of any possible value for commercial development, liability for inheritance taxes is reduced; but town taxes are unlikely to be affected favorably, since the owners have secured amenities for themselves in the assurance of unspoiled land.

In any case, experience shows that most of us who are in a middle-income group must be reluctant to devalue our land even by so well-intentioned an instrument as a conservation easement, since it is one thing to own land we do not want to sell, and quite another to own land we can't sell to advantage in case of some unforeseen desperate emergency.

The attitude of town assessors is also likely to be unpredictable, and no leniency on the part of a present board can forestall possible severity on the part of a future board. It is not only an economic fact but also a political fact that an increase in assessed valuations makes possible a lower tax rate, and that higher valuations here and there affect relatively few people, whereas lower taxes brought about by increased assessments are a boon to the electorate at large.

Assessors — and others — are likely to share the old-time faith that land should be built upon in order to "broaden the tax base," ignoring the fact that the demand for schools, roads, water, lighting, police, and so on through the list of services, inevitably makes developments expensive rather than advantageous to the town.

During the campaign for funds for the Wasque reservation a prominent Island official remarked, "All that land shouldn't be kept open. Part of it should be built on." And an old-time errant conservationist expressed the judgment that only the land around the ponds at Squibnocket should be preserved, and the rest built in order to "bring ratables" into the township. It will be long before this point of view is lived down.

There is wishful talk about favorable assessments for agricultural land, but in terms of plain realism such consideration is bunkum, amounting to nothing at all.

Among the imponderables is the blindness of proprietors to the consequences of land sales in which they are concerned. An island group, otherwise a model of wise environmentalism, sold extensive acreage at Christiantown without restrictions, and in a short time it became a development. One of the corporate group said, "Oh they didn't think." An excellent phrase for an obituary of the Vineyard: "They didn't think."

But such an instance is not exceptional. Large properties have been sold out of pique, others because of lack of further interest, still more avowedly for gain. Land ownership under the conditions of generations past tended to be stable; now it tends to fluidity and change, with preservation in a state of high risk.

One large tract of open land visible from a main Island highway, typical of those offering long vistas and sightly contours, has been appraised at a value of a million dollars. The owner does not want to sell. This property has been in his family for a hundred years. Unusual is the fact that he does not forbid trespassing but maintains the old Island view of freedom in coming and going.

He receives no want of good advice. Well-wishers and government departments are overflowing with it. Conservationists organized and individually earnestly desire to help, but nothing is any good. How can such a region be kept intact under an old family ownership? It can't be. The old order has gone forever.

Zoning, prevailing at last over long and stubborn opposition — "We've got a right to do what we like with our own" — has come too late for the effectiveness it was intended to have. Population pressures and economic pressures teach the lesson that where there is, say, one-acre zoning today,

there is likely to be half-acre zoning ten years from now, or even much sooner.

To more obvious pressures is added that of a proper social awareness and conscience: "There must be some way for young people to acquire land. Not only the young, but also other segments of society should not be excluded. Land is not only for the rich and cultured and those who happen to have inherited properties too large for their own use."

Where may one look for wisdom in the use and preservation of land? That innovative regional authority, the Martha's Vineyard Commission, is fought and checkmated. A native and insular reluctance to part with any right or power is joined to a political instinct for keeping control within power centers in the towns, centers likely to be favorably inclined toward variances, a relaxing of restrictive regulations, and some degree of co-operation with entrepreneurs who are persuasive about economic benefits to the town.

The Steamship Authority, conceived out of necessity as an instrumentality that would operate for the economic benefit of the Islands, is engaged in the promotion of mass tourism because this is the most profitable part of its business and because of the competition of excursion lines, although such a policy runs counter to the expressed will of a majority on the Islands and is rapidly changing the character of Island life. Any change, if it can be brought about at all, is unlikely to be brought about soon.

How long can images like this last?

The West Tisbury swan pond —
a tourist attraction

After World War II few Island leaders were left who were born in the nineteenth century, few who could remember when automobiles were few, or could recall an era without airplanes, or who had lived as children without television and its influence, among whatever else, toward conformity of living.

Some years ago I wrote: "An unprecedented transition period had slipped into the past, during which automobiles had replaced horses, bathrooms had replaced privies, and cardboard cartons seemed to have replaced cows. . . . What we noticed was the almost complete change in the roles of leading town figures — no longer the skepticism as to 'progress,' no more the strongly asserted individual opinions in the vein we had known, no more the superstitions and familiar doubts. . . ."

These last we had deplored, but now we realized that they were an oblique but important contribution to the formation of community opinion. Better by far were they than assumptions originating in corporate public-relations departments and insinuated into decision-making.

For three centuries the character of the Vineyard drew upon all regions of the earth, at the same time maintaining a culture and homogeneity based upon the relationship of husbandry on land and enterprise along shore and at sea. Productivity was related to the seasons, insularity, and natural resources.

Traditionally the Island had tested the ideas of the outside world against its own view. As it now appears, suddenly the historic character was changed. A new character and a new culture had emerged in response to modern influences, and the Island tested its ideas against the views of the outside world.

Martha's Vineyard, like the rest of the Western world, had slipped over into the era Dr. Daniel Bell has termed an age of wants rather than needs, and of "entitlements."

A good while ago August Hecksher wrote: "The result of technological forces — combined with increased numbers of people, increased wealth, increased mobility, and increased leisure — is to threaten the existence of every geographical place which is separate and distinct, every integrity which gives to the individual the possibility of standing apart and meeting the world on his own terms."

Applying the obvious truth of this to the Vineyard, one may find a grain of comfort in being convinced that our decline could not have been helped, is really not of our own making.

The last surge of decentralization-*cum*-individualism occurred during the Great Depression, which was not all bad. The new decentralization is a web of central ownership, often with some conglomerate over and above, related to small, scattered outlets in any of several ingenious modern patterns. It would be idle to assume that this national change has had no effect on the Vineyard, even if one could not remember how Island individualism in culture and economics used to be.

It is more important now to consult the plans of the developers than the plans of any elected or appointed Island bodies or agencies. The ultimate decision does not lie ahead; it has already been made, and the rest of the way will be only going down.

I will wrench from an entirely different context these lines from Swinburne because I like them and because the state of Martha's Vineyard requires a requiem charged with deep emotion:

> There is no help, for these things are so,
> And all the world is bitter as a tear.

Henry Beetle Hough was born in New Bedford but was brought to the Vineyard in 1898 at the age of two. His boyhood summers were spent in North Tisbury when a trip to Vineyard Haven was a major event, requiring an hour and a half behind an agreeable farm horse. He and his wife settled in Edgartown in 1920 and since then Mr. Hough's life has revolved around newspaper work and writing. The newspaper is the Vineyard Gazette *(he still writes all the editorials), and the writing includes novels, histories, reminiscences, and memoirs, of which* To the Harbor Light *(1976) is the most recent.*

The Oak Grove Farm in Chilmark is one of a handful of farms to resist development.

Two well-preserved Chilmark homes

Marianne Wiggins, at home and in view

"AND TO YOUR LEFT, LADIES AND GENTLEMEN, MY HOUSE!"

Marianne Wiggins

My house sits in the middle of a meadow along what is referred to vaguely in the deed as a "Massachusetts State Highway," which is another way of saying "paved," a term loosely applied to the streets of Heaven and generally accepted as the surface best suited to roller-skating, traffic cops, and tour buses.

Let me explain: I don't buy a lot of houses. I don't have as much experience picking houses as I do, say, cantaloupes. I know to count the sockets. I once rented a secluded house for writing in Vermont that had plenty of electric current, no place to plug into it. I know to count the closets, too, another helpful hint from one of my bum rentals. I know to check the flues: These worked, next fireplace I check, I'll know to pack Visine. I checked the plumbing, drank a glassful of the tap water, knocked on walls, and bought the place. It has a great room, bright and airy with a skylight off the bedroom for my writing. Flynn, the realtor, seemed pleased. Spring on the Vineyard, he advised me, is always lovely. I nodded. The crabapple trees along the gravel driveway were in bloom. "Are you sure your family won't be bothered being so close to the road?" he asked me.

How quaint, I thought. A little country road in Chilmark. How quaint of Flynn to ask. "Why?" I kidded him: "Is South Road a parade route?"

I was so green a prospect, Flynn's radar must have gone berserk when I got off the ferry.

"Sometimes in the summers you'll find some people take this road out to Gay Head," he mentioned, nonchalantly.

Summer, then, seemed like a distant prospect.

It arrived, by busload, the first weekend in July.

The little driveway leading to the little country road seems shorter, now that days are longer, and I refuse to post it "PRIVATE" owing to my perverse belief that driveways, in and of themselves, lead off, like linen closets from a corridor, and I would no more explore the closet shelves of strangers than wander down their driveways, but I am oddly quaint and embarrassingly shy and wouldn't drive a red Volkswagen van, anyway, with stickers from Luray Caverns and the Alaskan Highway and bring all four kids, one of whom has a rampant case of poison ivy and has to use the bathroom, to the kitchen door explaining, "Hi, your house was on the tour, we're leaving Friday, we're from Bushkill Falls, Sonny's in the roofing business, mind if we take a little look around?"

I'm a stranger here, myself. I say: "What tour?"

The Bushkill eyes fall on my well-worn bathrobe and peer beyond me to the table set for breakfast.

"I just bought the place: What tour?!" I repeat.

"Just bought it, huh?" Sonny muses. He cranes his neck around the ivy-covered porch to inspect, no doubt, the roof and asks: "What'd it go for?"

The only thing I'm wearing that could be described as fitting tightly is a smile and I hitch it up securely in the corners and reply, "A song."

"Well, it sure is pretty," Wife-of-Sonny says. "They told us on the tour bus it used to be a horse barn."

"Dairy," Sonny prompts.

"Horse."

"Cows, I told ya."

"Horse!"

I hate family quarrels. "Camels," I put forth to end the matter.

"Daddy, look," Son-of-Sonny interjects. "I found a kitten. . . ."

Later that same morning, my daughter tells me one of our cats is missing and I expound without effect on the quixotic roamings of the male, only to be interrupted by the appearance at the front door of two blithe spirits who announce, "Hi, your house was on the tour—"

My smile, along with my trusty bathrobe and the cat is, at this point, loosed.

"Is it true this was the only stable on the Island?" I am asked. I'm told they ride. I am not comforted. I have an Arab gelding. True, keeping pets can be expensive, but I'm already down one cat from the morning's previous encounter. Would I come out and take their picture petting my horse on my front lawn? As I point their Pentax at them, the tour bus lumbers by: "Here to your right is an example of—" The rest is lost. Did George Washington sleep here? Did his horse? I am asked if my horse had to come across on the ferry. The question leaves me speechless. I contemplate explaining there was once a bluegrass isthmus that connected Chilmark to Hialeah, but I'm thwarted by a caravan of cyclists who, encouraged by the sight of people in the driveway, want to know if they can leave their cycles on the lawn and try to hitch a ride from passing motorists whose cars have the magic Lucy Vincent Beach stickers. "You own this place?" they ask.

I nod.

"You got a car?"

I nod, again.

"You got a Chilmark resident's beach sticker for restricted beaches on it?"

"Yeah."

"Can we use it?"

"The sticker?"

"No, the car."

"Sorry, I just loaned it out to Walter Cronkite."

"Well," they shrug. "Cool house, anyway."

"Thanks."

"It's on the tour," they tell me.

Funny, the way even strangers notice things about a house that listing realtors somehow overlook. I begin to wonder what Sonny found so interesting about the roof.

Between uninvited guests, I go upstairs to change. Glancing from my bedroom window, I notice a large man standing in the center of the yard taking a picture of the house. He sees me at the window, lowers his camera, and waves at me to step away. I oblige. I, myself, can sympathize with the disconcerting intervention of strangers in a snapshot, an occurrence certainly more aesthetically appalling than the appearance of strangers on one's lawn. If one is a serious photographer, that is, and has a handle on perspective and talks about putting things in their proper light. Development, I tell myself, is a term common to both picture-taking and real estate; as subdivision is to property and cellular disease. There are moments, when the tour bus passes, I think longingly of Levittown.

As we are sitting down to lunch, a man with a broken foot and a cane comes to the door, explaining that he is looking for a house to rent next summer and he's always been in love with this one and he's just fallen into a lot of money so no matter what the price is, he'll take it, and when I ask if falling into fortune is how he suffered his infirmity, he responds, not humorously, "Well, how about the winter, then?"

"Taken," I say.

"Oh? By whom?"

"By meem. And mine."

"Oh. I see. One of those," he says. "Locals."

I always fancied "natives" was somehow a nicer word: more savage.

At lunch, we look out at the buses slowing so the passengers can snap their photos. "Smile!" my daughter says. We smile, saying hissy things behind our teeth. Sometimes we wave. Sometimes we even wonder what our faces will look like on all those home screens. Sometimes I'm obsessed with the idea of a moat.

If I build a little moat around it, my home could be an island to itself. Islands, I've been told, are blessed by pleasant natives, fragrant breezes, and the gift of solitude. With my luck, my moat would strike some hapless crew as a great location for a movie. Besides, when I asked Flynn if he could find me a used drawbridge, he said: "Are you sure your family won't be bothered by a few small floodlights near the toll booths?"

Marianne Wiggins, a distinguished novelist, lives year round in Chilmark. Her house is not for sale. In July and August it is leased to the Vineyard Center for the Study of Contagious Diseases. Her latest book Went South, *is to be published by Delacorte Press in July 1980.*

Island patriotism.

Good fences
make good tourists.

THE ART OF LOAFING
James Reston

A **great many people** come to Martha's Vineyard in the summertime to loaf, but if you watch them working and struggling at their rest, it is obvious that the art of creative loafing in America is on the decline.

The trouble seems to be that, not counting the millions of welfare loafers and the millions more who are out of work as involuntary loafers, most people underestimate the difficulty of being idle.

I have been taking lessons from the great prophets of idleness, and I must tell you they are not much help. "It is impossible," says Jerome K. Jerome, "to enjoy idling thoroughly unless one has plenty of work to do." I never met Mr. Jerome, but obviously he never lived under the tyranny of a newspaper deadline or idled joyfully past edition time.

Most of the old masters merely tease us with assertions or descriptions of the glories of idleness but never tell us how to achieve them. Tacitus talks about the "sweetness of being idle." Pliny the Younger, as distinguished from my colleague Finney the Elder, raves on about "that indolent but delightful condition of doing nothing."

Ralph Hodgson, who apparently has a pipeline to

Sack-out time on the soft shoulders of Old County Road

the Almighty, assures us that "God loves an idle rainbow no less than laboring seas," and then, of course, there are all those killjoys who insist that the Devil picks up more recruits among the idle and indolent than anywhere else.

Walt Whitman at least suggests one practical approach to the problem. "I loafe and invite my soul, I lean and loafe at my ease observing a spear of summer grass," he says in *Song to Myself.* So I took my soul out to Cedar Tree Neck the other day, and leaned and loafed with three other idle seekers, and invited my soul, and inspected a great many spears of grass, but nobody answered but the ticks and mosquitoes.

Accordingly, I have been forced to devise a system of my own, and offer it here as the first installment of my *Loafer's Guide to Martha's Vineyard.* First, I wake up at seven twenty-five in the morning and tune in WCBS News from New York just in time to miss all the main news but precisely and solely to hear the helicopter reports on the traffic.

As soon as I hear that the traffic is backed up from the Triborough Bridge to La Guardia Airport, the Long Island trains are all stalled in tunnels, and the subways have come to a complete stop, I roll over happily and go back to sleep. This I repeat on a Boston station at seventeen minutes to nine, and when the Mystic Bridge is hopelessly snarled, I rise betimes and dress in the rattiest old outfit I can find.

After breakfast I used to have a problem wondering about what to do about inflation. But now after practicing for two weeks, my only problem is whether NOT to read about it in the *Boston Globe* or NOT to read about it in *The New York Times.* On the whole I tend to favor not reading about it in the *Times* because it prints more on inflation and thus enables me to miss more than by not reading about it in the *Globe.*

In addition to inflation, other topics to be avoided during the summer holiday season are the plight of the Democratic Party, the plight of the Republican Party, the future of Gerald Ford, the problems of nuclear energy, the whereabouts of Henry, the tendency of the Red Sox to collapse after the All-Star game, Watergate, China, Nixon, Carter, Senator Kennedy, Ronald Reagan, the stock market, woman's liberation, sharks, and the sex habits of the young.

Idle talk on these subjects is less fun than watching kids shake apples out of the trees and is guaranteed to interfere with the joys of idleness. Sailing, fishing, tennis, and other games can be diverting, but golf is a curse invented by the Scots as a punishment for the sins of the human race. Nothing is to be gained by hacking around the bunkers or fussing over the CIA or any of these other avoidable irritations.

A moment's meditation

Carly Simon, mowing leisurely

They will all be in precisely the same pickle in the fall, except that the Red Sox may win this time. Pascal once said that many of the troubles in the world came from our inability to sit quietly in a room. Idleness and even indolence, Walter Bagehot thought, were often better than excessive activity, a point recently forgotten in Washington.

The characteristic American heroes of the past, Mark Sullivan argued, were not the hustlers, but the whittlers, but whittling, like reading, has gone out of style, and the pessimists have taken over.

The welfare state has given "loafers" a bad name, and vice versa, but creative loafing is something else. It is a time for not having to do things at a time certain, like writing columns when you don't have to, but some of us have lost the art, even on Martha's Vineyard.

"To do nothing is to be nothing," thought Nathaniel Howe. So did Johnson and Nixon, and look what happened to them!

James Reston, copublisher with his wife of the Vineyard Gazette, *is a summer resident of Edgartown. His column from Washington for* The New York Times *is a mainstay of the Op-ed page. Mr. Reston also writes an occasional column for the* Gazette *called "Sketches in the Sand." He is now a director of the* Times *and attempts to loaf as much as possible, without much success.*

A slow-paced profession

Artful loafing, or creative occupation?

*Peaceful reading on
a hot and hazy afternoon.*

CIRCLES IN TIME — A VINEYARD REMINISCENCE

Evelyn Ames

In **the autumn** of 1973, our car, like that of many another summer resident of Martha's Vineyard, returned to the mainland sporting a big sticker that read "SAVE THE BUMP!" To puzzled off-Islanders, trying to construe this as some odd, safe-driving slogan, it had to be explained that the "bump" was the top of a hill on the historic Takemmy Trail, traveled by the Gay Head Indians, which — for safety reasons — airlines serving the Island wished to level off. The hue and cry that went up, verbally and in the pages of the *Vineyard Gazette,* became as fervent as all Vineyard issues are apt to do and, historic interest aside, the road itself is singularly appealing — running straight as the road in a child's drawing, uphill and down over a succession of small hills and valleys, extending across the landscape like a smoothly unrolling ribbon.

Still . . . any improvement wanted by Northeast, or Delta, or Executive — whichever airline it then was — seemed reasonable and desirable: anything to facilitate some of those landings in marginal weather conditions and set us safely down in that world beyond the world that we had come to treasure. However loyal to the Vineyard we were in buying the sticker and putting it on our car, we had ambivalent feelings.

Except for me. For very personal reasons I wanted no one, ever, to touch that bump, for it was on the Takemmy Trail that I had learned to drive a car. Although I was still too young to apply for a license, my father thought that utterly straight dirt road, with no side roads, then, between Edgartown and West Tisbury and rarely another vehicle, was an ideal place to teach me to steer and shift. Which of course it was, until the day he wanted me to downshift from third without stopping, and I unfathomably managed to go into reverse — ignominiously and with hideous sounds and jerks — suddenly backing up (no doubt) the bump itself. The memory makes me shudder for the old air-cooled Franklin I was driving — one of several cars that my father kept and ran for fifteen years and more: "It gets me there, doesn't it? Why should I turn it in, as you put it, for a new, and less good, car?"

The landscape along the trail looked very different in that summer of 1924. The disastrous forest fire of 1916 was still recent enough so that the land was all a kind of blasted heath with only an occasional dwarf oak raising its leaves above the dismal, scrubby level of the rest. Somewhere in that heath, the last heath hen on earth was managing to survive. I don't believe I am phantasizing when I remember — just once — seeing it from the car on one of our expeditions up-Island.

That summer and the one before it were my brother's and my first on the Vineyard; our parents had come a year earlier "to try it out" and fell in love with the Island. We lived in rented houses in Edgartown, which, aside from the very few automobiles and far fewer shops (and people) was remarkably like today, so much so that it is quite eerie to walk along those same lovely streets now — past gardens and picket fences and rose-bowered porches — recognizing most of them, feeling that no time at all can have passed. In today's world? How is it possible?

But Edgartown activities have indeed changed a lot, including the sailing. We bought a Wareham-built Cape Cod sailing dory in which my brother and I raced (and won the season trophy the second summer). That class of eight or nine boats; a class of Herreshoff 15s and one of "Wianno boats" (I'm not sure what they were) were the only sailboats competing in the harbor, while the number of visiting cruising boats was so small that a new arrival was an event and we hurried out to row around it and have a look. There was no Yacht Club building as such; after races, the Race Committee met on someone's porch that overhung the harbor, and crews sailed up to make their protests and have them adjudicated. Races were started, timed, and followed by a small launch, and since the dories capsized easily and the afternoon southerlies were as apt as now to be very brisk, quite a few wet sailors were picked up and taken on board. A hero of the class was a slight, quizzical-faced boy named Whit Griswold, who once climbed the mast in the middle of a race to rerig a broken main halyard. I thought he was wonderful. And a great event, for me, was to have a handsome boy with a reputation for sailing skill, named Jerry (for Jared) Bliss, invite me for an afternoon sail in his Herreshoff 15.

Then, as now, one swam from a beach at the near end of Chappaquiddick — from what was called Chadwick's Beach. The manager and proprietor of the bathhouses was a Dickensian tyrant whose arbitrary rules some friends and I once flouted — to our disgrace. Certain clothing ("swimwear" was a term not even dreamed of) was not only expected but also required: For boys and men it was swimming trunks and what we would now call a tank top; for women and girls, an undergarment in the form of a close-fitting, black, and knit-in-one-piece union suit named after the leading female swimmer of the day, an "Annette Kellerman"; over this a "bathing dress," short-sleeved, reaching down to the knees and usually with two or three flounces at hem and cuff. But — this was still not

The Edgartown United Methodist Church

*A dune at Zack's Beach —
now off limits*

enough! One was also required to wear long, black stockings — rolled *above* the knee (quite a trick to keep them up there), and bathing shoes. Why the last is hard to imagine, unless the formidable Mr. Chadwick didn't want to be sued for splinters or stubbed toes?

How did we ever swim? And how — when in the often flirtatious roughhousing out on the float, a girl was tossed into the water by some boys, did she ever come to the surface? I suspect that my lifelong distrust of being underwater, and never learning to dive, stem from that time and that forbidding figure who actually banned us from the beach for a couple of weeks for appearing with stockings rolled *below* the knees.

Two other quite famous Edgartown institutions have vanished: Manuel Silva's wonderful boat shop — the true club for sailors of all ages — and, of course, Manuel himself; and the town idiot, known as Lenny the Horse — for that was what he believed he was and what he came to resemble with his inevitable trotting gait through the streets, the odd bone formation of head and face, and his delight and usefulness in carrying and delivering goods, sometimes in a little cart with shafts in which he ran as if he were in fact a horse.

Aside from sailing and swimming and picnics,
the pleasantest diversions of those summers were our up-Island expeditions. On the dirt roads and in our elderly car, that is what they were, even without the special sense of adventure given them by my father who, all his life and anywhere in the world, loved "exploring" and who had made genuine explorations in Iceland and was a member of the Explorers' Club. There were few back roads, stretches of beach, or approaches to the Island's ponds we didn't explore. A favorite *bout de promenade* was Priscilla Hancock's shop in Quansoo to buy her marvelous candy; another was the Hawaiian Tea Room, a small and charming place with a wall of windows overlooking Lagoon Pond where one could enjoy not only afternoon tea but dinner as well. (What ever happened to "tea rooms"? No coffee shop or snack bar can possibly replace the gentle and restorative atmosphere of those unpretentious places — unspoiled as yet by jukeboxes, Muzak, or transistor radios.) But our favorite expedition of all was an evening picnic at Lake Tashmoo. I don't know who owned the eastern shore of the lake, though it is my impression that it was all held by the water company; in any case, there were no houses at all. Leaving the car beside the road and walking a little way through the woods, we settled ourselves on the shore and ate our supper, watching the sunset sky turn the surface of the lake one opalescent shade after another until the stars began to appear in the

*Man-made patterns meld
into a Vineyard backdrop*

A bucolic frame from Gay Head.

Snooze time aboard the Raison d'Etre,
anchored in Menemsha

luminous darkening blue and my father pointed out to us the summer constellations and first-magnitude stars.

The second of those summers there was an August hurricane which, though nowhere nearly as catastrophic as the one of 1938, nevertheless caused tremendous local damage. Right after it, and very exciting for us as a family — my father's brother, a medical missionary in China, came to visit us. He loved the Island at once and in later years was to spend many holidays there when he was on leave, but on that first visit he was anxious to find a really quiet spot where he might stay for some time to recover from a minor heart ailment. He found it; he wanted us all to see it. I remember the drive up-Island on the North Shore; then miles of small bumpy roads winding through moorland and sheep pastures (some with gates that had to be opened and reclosed); finally our destination: Obed Daggett's. We met Obed himself, a stolid-looking, taciturn man; we walked to the shore of a pond, on the edge of which we were shown the gray-shingled, one-room cabin that Uncle Edward would be occupying for the next two or three months. Off the end of a little dock, two planks

wide, an ancient rowboat was tied, resting on its upside-down image, softly kissing and rising from it with the gentle movement of the water. It was a gray afternoon, suffused with premonitions of autumn, and I was filled with a sense of loneliness and desolation. I wondered how Uncle Edward would endure it.

My next return to the Vineyard was not until eighteen years later, in May of 1942. The United States was at war and my husband, Amyas, was about to go to Washington to work in the War Shipping Administration: We wanted to have a vacation first, and spent this in Edgartown, at the Charlotte Inn. Gasoline rationing had already begun; we bicycled everywhere, over the still winter-cool Island, past gardens whose tulips and lilacs were weeks behind our own at home, on Long Island; through almost bare woods where the oaks were thickly hung with tassels, the leaves no more than small, rosy stars.

Anne Lindbergh, one of my closest friends, was living with her children at Seven Gates Farm at the time, in the old Webb house, and invited us to come over for the night. Charles being at Willow Run, helping to speed up our production of bombers,

Lake Tashmoo

Cedar tree neck

she was quite lonely for adult company and eager to show us the lovely place to which they had fled from unwanted intrusions. After tea, she and I walked a woodland path down to the beach — coming out at a point no more than a quarter of a mile from where, fourteen years in the future, we would be building the house in which we have summered every year since. The oddness of thus brushing the fringes of our future, like rubbing shoulders in a crowd with the person one is going to marry, stays with me. Do such events perhaps happen more often on islands? On Martha's Vineyard more often still?

We built our Vineyard house; we walked the beaches, enjoying especially the one leading to Cedar Tree Neck. We understood that our friend J. Donald Adams, whom we had met through Anne Lindbergh and whose column "Speaking of Books" in *The New York Times Book Review* was a weekly pleasure, summered there. We were delighted when he and his wife invited us over for dinner. They gave us drinks in a tiny cottage that was one of several scattered around the central farmhouse where everyone in the inn community had meals. But first,

Donald led us down a path from their cabin to see the pond — and there, like a picture slipping out from the pages of an old book, appeared the scene I already knew so well: the gray-shingled cabin, the two-plank dock, and the single rowboat of my uncle's retreat. In the rich summer evening sunlight, and with ripples dancing on the water, it looked not at all forlorn but inviting.

We went to dinner. A pigeon-breasted, intrepid-looking woman with a deepish voice greeted us, and we were introduced to Miss Emma Daggett. I sat next to her at the table and taking a long chance asked her, "Did you ever know an uncle of mine, Miss Daggett? His name was Dr. Edward Perkins." She turned halfway around in her chair and fixed me with an unforgettable look. "*Know* him?" she almost shouted, "I have a small *trunk*ful of letters from him upstairs!"

Another circle completed. There have been others, just as there are sure to be many more that will describe their mysterious arcs, connect beginnings and endings and tie knowns and

The West Tisbury Church

The Dr. Daniel Fisher house

unknowns together. Whatever acausal forces are at
work in our lives, they achieve their unexpected
ends — to our astonishment and, often, to our
delight.

Martha's Vineyard — like Naushon and Bermuda
and who knows how many other islands — has
been suggested as being the island of Shakespeare's
Tempest. Perhaps. What seems certain is that there
is, on the Island, as in Shakespeare's play, a kind of
dance: of appearances and meetings, of partings
and returns — maybe even mysterious music — all
as unpredictable as those of Alonso and Sebastian,
of Ferdinand and Miranda. "Now I will believe that
there are unicorns!" exclaims Sebastian, and who,
on Martha's Vineyard, has not at one time or
another had the same feeling?

*Evelyn Ames, a summer resident of the Vineyard
for twenty-six years, lives at Seven Gates Farm on
the North Shore above Vineyard Sound. She is a
poet and novelist, author of* Daughter of the
House, *a memoir novel:* A Glimpse of Eden, A
Wind from the West *(Bernstein and the New York
Philharmonic abroad), and most recently,* In Time
Like Glass *(Reflections on a Journey in Asia). Her
poems have appeared in many magazines, and
she has been a frequent contributor to the*
Vineyard Gazette.

NO EXIT
FROM EDEN

Stan Hart

The Vineyard was always my safety zone or fall-back spot — a place I could retreat to with assurance that everything was really okay. I don't know exactly when the Island took on such a guardian role, but I would suspect it was during my thirteenth year when we moved from New Britain, Connecticut, to southern Maryland. I believe it was at that time when I began to feel that Maryland didn't count, that only the Vineyard counted.

I began to feel that as long as the Island existed I had roots, a base, and, in a sense, an identity. This meant, alas, that what I did in Maryland, and later on in Connecticut, New York, California, or Boston was essentially of little consequence, just the filling of an interlude until I could get home to the Vineyard. And so it was with secondary school, college, the U. S. Air Force, and two good jobs. They were ancillary activities that didn't really matter — the main thing was always there on the Vineyard.

Undoubtedly the Vineyard's pervasive hold on me reflects a youth spent summer after summer, free in the sunshine, if you will, somehow nurtured by the Island's myriad blessings in those prewar years. And nurtured as I was by nature, and simplicity, by fresh air, sun and sea, and a summer house, I felt unique in those days and quite tenacious in my knowledge that I always belonged to the Vineyard.

And it *was* unique. It was a unique adventure coming every summer to Martha's Vineyard. I remember the route down from New Britain, Connecticut, and the dock in New Bedford where we would board either the *Nantucket,* the *New Bedford,* or the *Naushon.* There was a smell to the wharf area, a very salty odor, and the water between the steamer and the dock was slime green and very still like green paint before it's stirred. The giant hawsers that tied the steamer to the pilings smelled of oil and grease and I would stand on the deck at the railing, staring at the cool green water waiting for the sudden whoosh of prop wash, which would tear its placid surface with white foam. Soon, then, the hawsers would go slap into the water, cast loose but falling short of the dock. It would be early June, and we would be off, easing out of our berth on our way to the Vineyard, the fresh smell and taste of ocean air easing over and into the ship.

There was nothing routine about this. You did not just drive down to Woods Hole and hop on an ugly beetle-shaped ferry as you do now. On those old steamers with their mahogany interiors you "booked passage" — quite another thing from buying a ferry ticket. But what made it most memorable was that in those days before the war and right afterward, it seemed that everyone's face on board was familiar and the odds were that you would know at least half of your fellow passengers. It *was* like coming home and you could feel a palpable camaraderie as people nodded to each other in recognition or shook hands warmly, it having been nine months or so since they had last met. People knew who the others were, and that sense of recognition was key to my early remembrances of the Island. For it was not just on the steamers and later the ferry *Islander,* but it was on land as well. For better or worse you had no anonymity here. Your face if not your name had been noted over the years, and as the years went by one was bound by a deep sense of belonging.

I remember rather subtle pleasures, too. The odor of sun-baked sand and beach grass and the run below the small bridge where Farm Pond enters into Harthaven Harbor, all this hitting me at once as we rounded the bend by the sea wall in Oak Bluffs on our yearly arrival. If New Bedford was an awakening this was a confirmation that we were once again really on the Island, the exquisite adventure already a fact. And later in the summer I would take my wooden toy sailboat, a replica of the

Anchored in Edgartown.

An irresistible ferry activity

Middle Road in spring

America's Cup defender *Rainbow,* and carry it down to Ocean Park in Oak Bluffs to float it in the wading pools, letting the wind catch the sails and watch the sailboat go careening off to bang up against the other side of the pool. Usually the waters before our house in Harthaven would be too ripply for the delicate balance of the J-boat, so I would walk on down to Ocean Park. I would dawdle on my way home, my large wooden sailboat askew under one arm, my feet scuffling the hot macadam of the black sidewalk that runs along Farm Pond. There was a pace to life back then in the thirties that was slow enough to allow for discovery. And if there were people around they were in such small numbers that they did not intrude upon one's imagination, did not hustle a boy away from his dreams.

And there were not that many of us, not so many summer residents that you couldn't keep track. We knew who was over in Edgartown and although West Chop was an enclave even then, I remember swimming up there a few times and occasionally I'd meet someone from that aloof promontory. In any case, I had seen West Choppers "around." Vineyard Haven and East Chop kids were far more

accessible, and I knew most of them. I also knew most of the Chilmark summer people, if only by their faces. Back in the forties and early fifties the summer colony in Gay Head was very small and too remote and there still were only a few houses along the North Shore. Indeed, when a friend of mine and I walked around the Island in 1947, the North Shore was mostly deserted. And at night sliding up the Sound with the running lights on in our Palmer Scott power boat you seldom saw house lights except at Seven Gates Farm and right around Tashmoo Inlet. The hills of Chilmark were, of course, barren of houses save for one here and there, belonging to some early visionaries who admired the rare beauty and the peace and quiet of that up-Island area.

And beauty there was. The up-Island South Beach, as an example, was heavy with beach grass and Sahara-like with its dunes and hollows. The upper and lower Chilmark ponds were connected by a navigable stream, which I used to canoe on moonlit nights. Slipping along those still waters right inside the edge of the ocean, I could hear the plangent thud of surf breaking on hard sand to my left and the rustling of herons in the marsh grass on my right. The mosquitoes could be awful but it was like finding a Northwest Passage slipping along those lambent waters. And when I entered upper Chilmark Pond it was always a discovery, consumed with raw nature, each ripple of the pond picking up the moonbeams, and the ocean white from the light above. I used to think then that I could never leave the Island no matter what. I would never leave to return to school or college or the Air Force or my job. But I always did, assuming that someday I would be back to stay.

We had cousins who owned two camps up on upper Chilmark Pond, and when I was a small boy my parents would take me along to parties at one or

A bit like Grand Central Station

*Childhood games on the flatlands
of Chilmark.*

the other of the shacks, as we called them. Before eating we would all row or paddle across to the ocean to swim in the big rolling surf and then, wet and sandy from being tumbled in the foam, we would return to warm ourselves before the fire. Neither shack had inside toilets and the cooking arrangements were very rudimentary, but we always ate very well and if nature called I would hurry down the walk to the outhouse, trying to avoid the prickers in the grass and the mounds of sheep dip that the grazing herd would have scattered all over the land. At night my parents would put me to bed in a loft up over the living room where I would sleep while they reveled below. The loft always smelled of mothballs and canvas and sometimes the fire would emit special oily fumes from the driftwood that someone

had collected from the beach. Lying up there pretending to sleep I would hear the grown-ups laughing and singing, singing songs from the Depression such as, "Let's Put Out the Lights and Go to Sleep," one line of which was, "No more parties at the shore, no more staying up till four." I think right then I knew I was in a special world. Others might not be having their parties at the shore, but we were. It seemed that the few of us who had the Vineyard had everything, and that neither a depression nor a war would ever change it.

But prosperity did. Prosperity and people and maybe your friendly banker who was happy to loan you the money for your summer house on beautiful, unspoiled Martha's Vineyard.

I do not know where I can go, should I leave this place. I have married the Vineyard for life and ruefully I admit that if there is any adjusting to be done it must come from me. Already I know that

*The Keith Farm
in Chilmark*

Glacial rock on South Beach

certain things that please my children so much are distasteful to me, my offspring already part of the present leading on to the future. I who look to the past, agonizing over the quality of life now departed, cannot become so immobilized as to lose track of those aspects that remain, those aspects still rewarding, still beneficial to man's well-being. And so I plod along, just a middle-aged man nursing the days of his youth.

I live on, year-round now, having moved here for keeps in 1968. I have a small bookstore and a home in Chilmark on property that I have owned for twenty years or so, land that was once my grandfather's. I live in seaside suburbia that for nine months of the year is deserted save for my family and two or three others. But in the summer they are all there, the eager newcomers who have been lured to the Island and who love it now as much as I do. Yet they don't know what they have missed, and probably happy with their own good fortune, they couldn't care less. And I appreciate them, for surely they are as blameless as they are lucky, just as I was lucky in 1930 when I first came over from New Bedford.

So it is a mixed bag. It is not the paradise I had known, held onto while away and suppressed tears over each September when I had to leave. But in the glorious autumn and in late spring there is a bounty that makes it all worthwhile. And in the winter months when I stroll through town I get that old sense of recognition I used to get in the summer. I feel that I know everyone and everyone knows me and that I am home and what I do here matters very much indeed.

Stan Hart has been a resident of Martha's Vineyard for fifty years (the last eleven, year-round). He worked in the publishing business for ten years, first with Duell, Sloan and Pearce in New York, and then with Little, Brown in Boston. Recently he has become an editor-scout for Delacorte Press. Since 1968 he has owned the Red Cat Bookstore in North Tisbury, also known as tennis central. Its hours are irregular, even challenging. He occasionally sells books, writes articles, and has written The Marthas Vineyard Affair *to be published in July 1980 by Dell. His regular features in the* Vineyard Gazette *have gained a deserved following.*

Sunshine daydreams

Mottled view

Day's end comes to Menemsha.

Winter solstice

A sail out in the sun on Lambert's Cove

LAMBERT'S COVE
Carly Simon

Out to the west of Lambert's Cove
There is a sail out in the sun
And I'm on board though very small
I've come home to stop yearning

Burn off the haze around the shore
Turn off the crazy way I feel
I'll stay away from you no more
I've come home to stop yearning

Carly Simon came to the Vineyard with her parents in the first year of her life. She has spent nearly every summer here since and moved here semipermanently in 1971. With her sister Lucy, she played at the legendary Mooncusser Cafe in Oak Bluffs in the midsixties. Her most memorable Island appearance was at the Martha's Vineyard No-nukes Festival in 1978. Carly is also a founder and partner of The Hot Tin Roof, an entertainment club on the Vineyard. In her nine albums for Elektra Records, there are many songs which have Vineyard references. The poem Lambert's Cove, *appeared as part of a song, "Terra Nova," on James Taylor's album,* JT.